ENGLAND AND THE FRENCH REVOLUTION

T

CONTEXT AND COMMENTARY

Series Editor: ARTHUR POLLARD

ENGLAND AND THE FRENCH REVOLUTION

Stephen Prickett

MACMILLAN
EDUCATION

First published 1989

Published by
MACMILLAN EDUCATION LTD
Houndmills, Basingstoke, Hampshire RG21 2XS
and London
Companies and representatives
throughout the world

Typeset by Wessex Typesetters
(Division of The Eastern Press Ltd)
Frome, Somerset

Printed in China

British Library Cataloguing in Publication Data
Prickett, Stephen
England and the French Revolution.
(Context and commentary).
1. English literature—18th century—
History and criticism   2. France—History
—Revolution, 1789–1799—Literature
and the revolution
I. Title   II. Series
820.9'006   PR448.F7
ISBN 0–333–38705–8
ISBN 0–333–38706–6 Pbk

Contents

Acknowledgements

Much of the background to this book lies in a course I taught over a number of years at the University of Sussex with historians of the period. To my friends and former colleagues, John Burrow, Maurice Hutt and Eileen Yeo I probably owe more than I am aware. To Marilyn Butler, Ann Hone, Iain McCalman and Björn Tysdahl I am grateful for ideas and further reading; to Karen Thompson I owe the discovery of a collection of original pamphlets of the time; from my present colleagues, Dagmar Eichberger, Fred Langman and above all Rosemary Foxton I have received invaluable criticism, advice and help. My secretary, Karina Pelling, has throughout been a model of good-temper and efficiency even under the most trying circumstances. Mrs Jocelyn Dawson has been invaluable in the proofreading. It is a pleasure to record my debts to all these and many more.

List of Plates

1. Jacques-Louis David, *The Oath of the Horatii*, 1785. Paris, Musée du Louvre. Courtesy of the Bridgeman Art Library.
2. Jacques-Louis David, *The Oath of the Tennis Court, 20th June, 1789*. Paris, Musée Carnavalet. Courtesy of the Bridgeman Art Library.
3. Jacques-Louis David, *The Death of Marat*, c.1794. Brussels, Musée Royal des Beaux-Arts. Courtesy of the Bridgeman Art Library.
4. Jean-Joseph-Xavier Bidauld, *View of the Town of Avezzano beside Lake Celano in the Kingdom of Naples*, 1789. Paris, Musée du Louvre. Courtesy of Photographie Giraudon.
5. Illustrations to *The House that Jack Built* by William Hone, 1819.
   i Frontispiece
   ii The Wealth
   iii The Vermin
   iv The Dandy of Sixty.
6. Frontispiece to *A Parody on the Political House that Jack Built* by M. Adams, 1820.
7. Frontispiece to *The Real Constitutional House that Jack Built*. Anon. 1820.
8. Frontispiece to *The Loyalists House that Jack Built*, Anon. 1820.

Editor's Preface

J.H. Plumb has said that 'the aim of (the historian) is to understand men both as individuals and in their social relationships in time. "Social" embraces all of man's activities – economic, religious, political, artistic, legal, military, scientific – everything, indeed, that affects the life of mankind.' Literature is itself similarly comprehensive. From Terence onwards writers have embraced his dictum that all things human are their concern.

It is the aim of this series to trace the interweavings of history and literature, to show by judicious quotation and commentary how those actually working within the various fields of human activity influenced and were influenced by those who were writing the novels, poems and plays within the several periods. An attempt has been made to show the special contribution that such writers make to the understanding of their times by virtue of their peculiar imaginative 'feel' for their subjects and the intensely personal angle from which they observe the historical phenomena that provide their inspiration and come within their creative vision. In its turn the historical evidence, besides and beyond its intrinsic importance, serves to 'place' the imaginative testimony of the writers.

The authors of the several volumes in this series have sought to intermingle history and literature in the conviction that the study of each is enhanced thereby. They have been free to adopt their own approach within the broad general pattern of the series. The topics themselves have sometimes also a particular slant and emphasis. Commentary, for instance, has had to be more detailed in some cases than in others. All the contributors to the series are at one, however, in the belief (at a time when some critics would not only divorce texts from their periods but even from their authors) that literature is the creation of actual men and women, actually living in an identifiable set of historical circumstances, themselves both the creatures and the creators of their times.

ARTHUR POLLARD

Author's Preface

With such a wealth of material available, any selection of documents concerning England and the French Revolution will at best appear arbitrary and incomplete. It seems proper, therefore, to acknowledge this at the outset and, given the limited space available, explain as well as I can the principles of selection. Certain writers – Price, Burke, Paine, for instance – are clearly indispensable for any account of the revolutionary debate within England (though it is important to note that two out of those three are not English) and it has been the intention to set such major political thinkers alongside the important literary figures of the period, such as Blake, Wordsworth, Coleridge, and later, Shelley. At the same time, I wished to give readers some sense of the diversity of the debate and an idea of the many different literary levels at which the argument was being conducted. Thus while Daniel Eaton, for instance, might publish both Southey and Shelley, it would be a mistake to think of the bulk of the political verse of the period or even in his journals as being of this standard or directed at this level of reader. Similarly William Hone is less well-known than he should be, and even those of his works commonly mentioned by histories of the period are often difficult to obtain. I have, therefore, included material from the (literally) thousands of pamphlets published during the period 1789–1820, among them Hone's liturgical parodies and *The Political House that Jack Built*, as well as others, like the anonymous *Death of Billy Cobb and Tommy Pain*, which have never to my knowledge been reprinted since they were first issued.

The principles of arrangement presented other problems. Should the material be arranged thematically, chronologically or simply by author? In the end I have chosen a compromise whereby the chapters are principally thematic, but within each chapter the writings cited are grouped under their authors in roughly chronological order. This has enabled me to concentrate on certain broad themes related in each case to the changing meanings of particular key words and their associated metaphors which emerge during the period, such as 'nature', 'revolution', 'enthusiasm' and the idea of the state as a work of architecture, which in turn reveal so much about the assumptions behind the revolutionary debate in England, while at the same time not separating the writings of any particular author from the context in which they were created.

The most controversial omission is probably that of Mary Wollstonecraft. Her *Letter to Burke* and *The Rights of Women* are of course important products of the revolutionary debate but the latter in particular is now easily available elsewhere, and they have reluctantly been left out in favour of other extracts from Charlotte Smith's much less well-known novel *Desmond*, as well as material from the letters and diaries of Fanny Burney.

Finally, what is implicit in the entire selection is spelled out in the last section linking Hannah More with Burke, Peacock and Carlyle; namely, that there is no way of dividing the debate over the Revolution in France from the subsequent radical agitations leading eventually to the Reform Bill of 1832 and beyond. It serves also as a reminder of the longevity and influence of the metaphors of such a debate, even in apparently non-political contexts, long after the situation that gave rise to them has disappeared or seemingly altered beyond recognition.

STEPHEN PRICKETT
Australian National University, Canberra, 1987

1 Introduction: Images of Revolution

There have been many revolutions – several even in France – but only one French Revolution. The events in France of the five years 1789–94, whatever their actual continuities or discontinuities with previous events there or elsewhere, were seen by the rest of Europe as something quite new in human experience. In October 1789 the novelist Fanny Burney wrote to her father, 'There is nothing in old history that I shall any longer think fabulous; the destruction of the most wonderful empires on record has nothing more wonderful, nor of more sounding improbability, than the demolition of this great nation, which rises up against itself for its own ruin – perhaps annihilation.' 'The French Revolution' conceded Burke a year later, 'is the most astonishing that has hitherto happened in the world.' Looking back at the end of his life, the radical publisher William Hone, born during the Gordon Riots in London in 1780, begins his memoirs with the statement: 'In the course of my brief life the most astounding events of modern times have happened. . . .' This book is specifically about the way in which the English in particular tried to come to terms with those wonderful and astounding events, both what they perceived to be happening to their near neighbours across the Channel, and increasingly with their consequences for their own society. It is therefore only concerned with the historical events of the Revolution as they affected the consciousness of contemporary English writers and commentators – and with the ways in which they attempted to *translate* those events into their own terms. What we shall be looking at, in short, are *ideas* or *images* of revolution. To use a fashionable word, it is about hermeneutics: that is, the study of how one particular society or culture interprets and assimilates ideas and ways of thinking originally generated in a quite different context.

It has been said that the French Revolution 'created the awareness of revolution' as a political phenomenon. In so doing, it produced a significant change of meaning in the word itself. Johnson's *Dictionary* of 1755 had defined the word 'revolution' primarily in terms of its original astronomical meaning, which implied the circular motion of an object that returned always to its original point. Its application as a metaphor to politics still retained this idea of circularity. Thus the English Civil War of 1649 was called the great *rebellion*; the Restoration of Charles II, on the other hand, was referred to as the *revolution* of 1660 because it meant a *return* to the Stuart monarchy. The supreme example, of course, present to all English minds in the early years of the French Revolution, was the 'Glorious Revolution' of 1688. The interposition of the new meaning of the word derived from the French experience of 1789 has now obscured for us the fact that, when the word was applied to the Revolution of 1688, it originally conveyed the sense that the expulsion of James II and the coronation of William and Mary, so far from being a change in political direction, was, in fact, a *restoration* of ancient liberties threatened by the tyrannical actions of James. Whatever may have been the intentions of some of those who took the famous Tennis Court Oath in Paris in 1789, however, or the interpretation given to the event by Richard Price in his commemorative sermon in London later the same year, there was by 1795 no way in which either French participators or English observers could pretend that what was in progress was a 'restoration' of anything. The word 'revolution' had acquired its new meaning of a clean break with the immediate political past. The nature and language of political debate had been irrevocably altered all over Europe.

The importance of this change cannot easily be over-estimated. Writing of the French Revolution debate, Ronald Paulson, has commented: 'We are dealing with poetic language and images that are self-generating in that they make little or no claim on the real world of what actually happened.' Such images of the Revolution, he argues, 'are complex, indefinite, and alogical, in contrast to the scientific language of the modern historian.' (Paulson, p.5). But this kind of confidence that we are privileged to know 'what actually happened' (presumably by the 'scientific' methods of the modern historian) suggests an oddly simplistic view both of history and of language. Knowledge is not separable from the perspective of the knower. If, as we have just seen, new experiences and the corresponding changes in consciousness they bring about are reflected by changes in language, such a separation between the actual events and the words and images used to interpret them is an illusion. The descriptions and images of the French Revolution debate conditioned the ways in which observers actually perceived those events. What to the republican, Tom Paine, was the justifiable fall of a tyranny was to Burke a violation of order and a threat to civilisation itself.

But merely to state the problem in this way is to invite at once a consideration not only of contemporary perspectives of the Revolution, but also of our own. Just as we shall be seeing the immediate English reactions to the first events of the Revolution in 1789–90 by such opposed figures as Burke and Paine in the light of the more considered reflections of the generation who grew up with the idea of the Revolution – Shelley, for instance, or, above all, Carlyle, so we must also be conscious of our own perspectives of the late 1980s. The editorial selection in a book such as this similarly reflects a particular interpretation of the period. More than that: our concern with trying to understand how and why contemporary English people understood the Revolution as they did is in itself indicative of late twentieth-century attitudes towards the writings of the past. There is no doubt that much of the current interest in the perspectives of the past stems from our own awareness that we ourselves are *also* conditioned by particular cultural perspectives, of which we may be hardly aware, to see things in certain ways – and therefore not in others. To a cultural historian of the twenty-first century our attitudes to the process of historical interpretation will themselves be part of the web of history and will require commentary and explanation – and will doubtless be the subject of debate and controversy. There is and can be no 'correct', definitive or final interpretation of any historical event of this nature, although there can be and are many that are demonstrably 'false' in the simple sense that they are unsupported by the known facts. Yet even here we must be

careful. Our selection of 'facts' is once again in part conditioned by the paradigm images we already hold about the
Revolution. As we have seen, the word 'revolution' itself
encapsulates one such paradigm image. Simply because of
that word, with its particular modern connotation, we
approach the events of the early 1790s with a certain set of
expectations.

For contemporaries, however, the paradigm images by
which they sought to explain the momentous events in France
were of a very different nature. James Woodforde, for
instance, who kept a diary throughout this period in his
country rectory in Norfolk, though apparently far removed
from what was going on in Paris was in fact no stranger to
mob violence. It was simply a fact of eighteenth-century life,
whether in England or France. He records with horror hearing
of the news of the execution of Louis XVI and Marie
Antoinette, but he also notes the 'king and country' anti-
radical riots in Birmingham, from which Joseph Priestley,
one of the foremost English scientists of the day, only just
escaped with his life. Woodforde himself in 1795 was caught
up in an even worse riot in London where the mob actually
attempted to kill George III. He does not use the word
'revolution' of events in either country.

Burke, of course, does: and it is to his *Reflections on the
Revolution in France* more than to any other single source
that we probably owe our modern meaning of the word. But
even here the word is used and justified with a certain sardonic
irony. He opens by referring to two London clubs, the
Constitutional Society and the Revolution Society, both of
which had apparently welcomed what Burke calls 'the late
proceedings in France' and gone so far as to send congratulatory addresses to the National Assembly in Paris. To a
modern ear the names of the two clubs might suggest that
they were at the opposite ends of the political spectrum, but
Burke assumes that his readers will recognise that in their
titles they are almost synonymous and hastens to add that he
too, as much as any man, shares the great political principles
which they were founded to uphold – those of the Glorious
Revolution of 1688. The whole thrust of his argument in
these first pages is devoted to showing that the gentlemen in

these clubs are quite mistaken in supposing that what they are witnessing in France is the emergence of a constitutional revolution to safeguard the liberty of its citizens on the English model. From the very first, therefore, the word 'revolution' is applied to the events in France only by what he sees as a monstrous mistake, and it carries throughout the force of a word in ironic quotation marks. By 1795, however, when Coleridge issued the prospectus for a series of lectures in Bristol on 'The English Rebellion and the French Revolution', the context suggests that the word had lost any such irony and acquired its modern meaning.

Other images, similarly, played a key part in contemporary perceptions of what was going on. For many French, reared in the classical tradition that has always been a strong element in Gallic education, the appropriate model was that of republican Rome with its suggestions of domestic virtue, stern patriotism and invincible destiny. This is an imagery made famous by, for instance, the early paintings of Jacques-Louis David, before he had become court painter to Napoleon. One thinks of *The Oath of the Horatii* (1784–85) or *Lictors returning to Brutus the Bodies of his Sons* (1789). This model not merely permitted the revolutionaries to think of themselves in terms of rugged republican virtue in defence of the motherland, but also had the added advantage of associating the *ancien régime* and its monarchist supporters with popular notions of the corruptions and degeneracy of the worst of the Roman emperors. Moreover, in the early days it enabled republicans to think of their achievements as 'revolution' in what we have seen was its original astronomical sense of a return to a previous golden age. But it is hardly surprising that, as the Revolution itself moved externally from defence to aggression, and internally from republican idealism towards factional struggles, purges and the Reign of Terror, images of the early days of the Roman Republic lost their appeal, and by 1793 the original vein of classical imagery was almost spent.

The changing fortunes of such images in the early 1790s illustrate in microcosm the turbulent history of the Revolution itself. Thus in one of the most potent visual expressions of the whole Revolution, David's painting of *The Tennis Court*

Oath, though the subject is contemporary rather than overtly historical, the classical ideology of David's earlier work persists in the formal, almost theatrical, plan of the original painting. This gigantic picture was commissioned by the Constituent Assembly in September 1791 to be hung, when finished, in its debating chamber. David thereupon invited all those who had participated in the original oath-taking to pose for him in his studio, and by the end of 1792 a number of portrait-studies were completed, as well as a sketch of the final composition, and work had begun on the central section (which alone measured four by six metres). By then, however, even such an official piece of propaganda could no longer keep pace with the rapid evolution of the political situation. Many of the central figures were politically suspect, had fled or been arrested, and the picture, which is now known to us only from preliminary sketches, was never to be completed. After the fall of Robespierre in 1794 David himself was twice arrested. The fate of his picture was to be symbolic of the failure of the visual iconography of classical republican fervour. Within two years we find David exploiting a very different kind of image in the thinly disguised and secularised religious imagery of *The Death of Marat*.

In this return to traditional religious imagery appears one of the two apparently unconnected models that were increasingly to dominate the visual and literary representations of the Revolution. The other can be seen, for instance, in a speech of La Fayette's to the National Assembly on 11 July 1789 (three days before the storming of the Bastille) and quoted with approval by Tom Paine at the beginning of the *Rights of Man*:

> Call to mind the sentiments which Nature has engraved in the heart of every citizen, and which take a new form once they are solemnly recognised by all: For a nation to love liberty, it is sufficient that she knows it; and to be free, it is sufficient that she wills it.

> Part I, p.282.

Such a semi-mystical faith in the power of Nature, once

recognised and so liberated, finds a visual counterpart in a painting of the same year by Jean-Joseph-Xavier Bidauld entitled *View of the Town of Avezzano beside Lake Celano in the Kingdom of Naples* where, in the towering mountains that dominate all evidence of man, a proto-Romantic kind of French landscape painting is beginning to emerge. Under the influence perhaps of such English painters as Alexander and John Robert Cousins, the classic style is charged with a new sense of the sublimity of nature and the pettiness of individual human endeavour. By implication, the Revolution was now to be compared with an elemental force of nature, or for its opponents an uprush of unconscious or even diabolic energies. In either case the new emphasis on collective action by 'the people' or 'the nation' as abstractions has the paradoxical effect of reducing by implication the individual's sense of controlling his own destiny which had been so central to older notions of freedom. If such imagery was becoming increasingly popular in France as a substitute for the metaphors of classical republicanism, we find that in England from the very beginning many pro-Revolutionary writers had been employing images drawn from nature and the natural world, often with similar implications of irresistible forces at work shaping human destiny. For Paine it forms one of the dominant images of Part II of *The Rights of Man*, which had been prepared for by earlier references to the Revolution as a new 'spring', while in one of the most famous passages of *The Prelude* Wordsworth says of the new mood of optimism that swept over himself and his radical contemporaries:

Bliss was it in that dawn to be alive
But to be young was very heaven!

Here, of course, juxtaposed with the natural metaphor of 'dawn' we find again that other strand of imagery that was to play such a significant, if subliminal, role in the English understanding of the Revolution – that of religious, biblical and apocalyptic events. For the young and idealistic the overthrow of the *ancien régime* was not so much the reflux of the natural as a no less irresistible breakthrough of the supernatural, a vision of heaven itself.

Though Wordsworth's enthusiasm for the Revolution was certainly extreme at this early stage, there was nothing particularly extreme or idiosyncratic in his imagery. To many British commentators, of all political persuasions, biblical and apocalyptic language seemed the obvious mode for describing such unprecedented events. Price uses it instinctively when he turns from the 1688 Revolution to consider what he sees as parallel events in contemporary France. Similarly, it is a marked feature of Burke's immediate response to the Revolution long before the execution of Louis and Marie Antoinette or the Reign of Terror, and it is equally present in the impressionistic rhetoric of Carlyle's history 40 years later. Though formal religious observance was possibly at its lowest ebb ever in England at the end of the eighteenth century, the generation that encountered the French Revolution was nevertheless one steeped in the Bible – able to use it, quote it and recognise even the most fleeting references or turns of phrase from the Authorised Version. Above all, it was a generation still emotionally in contact with the biblical framework of history.

What distinguishes the Old Testament from other documents of its time was its sense of change as a meaningful and not a random process, but this was not an idea of 'history' in the modern sense of that word. When the writers of the New Testament and the innumerable commentators that followed them in the first few centuries A.D. came to relate the events of the life of Christ and the early Church to those of the Hebrew Scriptures, they adopted as their hermeneutic principle a mode of historical interpretation that we now call 'typology'. According to this way of seeing events, even the most trivial or sordid happenings of the Old Testament were held to be 'types' or forecasts of some event of the New Testament, which was known as the 'antetype'. Even after Hume and Gibbon, for most ordinary people in the late eighteenth century there was no incongruity in using an 1800-year-old system of exegesis to explain the significance of the events of Old Testament narrative. The Bible was written by God himself and so might quite properly be treated as a single continuous work in which all the parts related to the whole.

But just as the New Testament served as the key to explain

the significance of the Old, so the Bible as a whole served as the key to explain all subsequent and previous history, which was, as it were, also a continuous divinely-ordered narrative from the beginning of the world to the Last Judgement. Though the scientific revolution of the seventeenth century and the Enlightenment had done something to undermine this traditional belief that momentous events could be directly attributed to God's actions, the typological interpretation of secular history died hard. It is very obvious in the political writings of Coleridge, for instance, and, as Kingsley's more professional colleagues were quick to observe, it was still present as late as 1860 in the latter's lectures on *The Roman and the Teuton*, given when he was Regius Professor of History at Cambridge.

Even where it is not visible as an explicit or even a consciously recognised principle, it is often still present in the imagery of a writer seeking to describe the impact of great events. Moreover, with the decay of a literal belief in the typology of history came an increased use of it as a fictional technique, especially in the popular form of the novel. What is often nowadays called 'symbolism' in the works of a novelist of our period, such as Jane Austen, should more properly be seen as typology – of a piece with the sermons she had heard every Sunday from her father throughout her childhood. In his early poem on the French Revolution, *The Destiny of Nations*, Coleridge uses the word in its latter sense, while at the same time psychologising and internalising it as a mode of consciousness:

> For all that meets the bodily sense I deem
> Symbolical, one mighty alphabet
> For infant minds.

ll. 18–20.

Similarly, Wordsworth's great interpretation of his own personal history, including his first-hand experience of the French Revolution, later to be known as *The Prelude*, is replete with a system of typology that relates the selected events of his early life to the growth of his mind as a poet. In this case such typology is largely (though not invariably) secular, but the inward and psychologised nature of his personal typology does not exclude a very real sense of a divinely-ordered exemplary scheme at work, not merely in the microcosm of his own life, but also in the macrocosm of the great political events of the day. Thus his comments on the news of the fall of Robespierre leave us in no doubt that what is in one sense as 'natural' as 'morning' coming 'out of the bosom of the night', is at the same time some kind of divine judgement.

> Great was my glee of spirit, great my joy
> In vengeance, and eternal justice, thus
> Made manifest. 'Come now ye golden times',
> Said I, forth-breathing on those open sands
> A hymn of triumph, 'as the morning comes
> Out of the bosom of the night, come ye . . .
> Elsewhere will safety now be sought, and earth
> March firmly towards righteousness and peace.'

Prelude (1805), Bk X, ll.539–44, 551–52.

Even where, as in the case of Carlyle, we can be sure the writer does not believe in any literal operation of divine judgement through history, the imagery of biblical typology persists and can be often much more obtrusive than in the philosophically reticent Wordsworth.

If we are attuned to such references (as frequently the modern ear is not), we often discover how apparently loose phrases are actually charged with quite specific referential meaning. For instance, Burke's description of the French people as the 'swinish multitude', which, as we shall see, was to become a catch-phrase of the whole Revolutionary debate in England, was not in fact a casual imputation of greed or dirtiness among the masses, but an allusion to the story of the Gaderene swine (*Matthew* 8, 30–32) who were possessed by devils and stampeded downhill into the sea where they were drowned. In the context where he uses it the reference becomes a pointed political parable of the leaderless mob. Indeed, so persistent and pervasive is biblical and typological imagery throughout the period of the Revolution and its aftermath that even conscious attempts to break away from it are not always successful. Paulson has pointed out, for instance, how much Mary Wollstonecraft's image of 'the people' as a 'vast elephant, terrible in his anger, treading down with blind fury friends as well as foes' draws on the biblical Behemoth (*Job* 40, 15–24) which is seen as essentially peaceful, but unstoppable when roused to use its strength.

More radical was Hone's deployment of biblical and liturgical images as satire from 1817 onwards. Turning with indignation upon the Lake poets who, he believed, had sold out to the establishment and substituted sanctimonious appeals to principle for action likely to lead to practical reform, he invoked a famous passage from the third chapter of *Daniel* where Nebuchadnezzar, King of Babylon, ordered his people when they heard the sound of the harp, the lute, the sackbut and the psaltery, to fall down and worship a golden image that he had created.

> And COLERIDGE shall have a Jew's Harp, and a Rabbinical Talmud, and a Roman Missal: and WORDSWORTH shall have a Psalter, and a Primer, and a Reading Easy: and unto SOUTHEY's Sack-but shall be duly added: and with Harp, Sack-but, and Psaltery, shall they make merry, and discover themselves before Derry Down Triangle, and HUM his most gracious Master whose Kingdom shall have no end.

Southey had by then been rewarded for his change of mind over the Revolution by being made Poet Laureate, among whose wages was included a butt of sack (or sherry, as it is now called). 'Derry Down Triangle' was Hone's name for Viscount Castlereigh, then the leader of the House of Commons, who was widely believed to have allowed a torture instrument called the 'triangle' to be used in the suppression of the Irish rebellion of 1798.

Such allusions and references – and they are too numerous to list – illustrate forcefully how much a society tends to use its traditional myths and views of the past as a means of interpreting current events, whether as the wrath of God or as material for satirists. Moreover, the more bewildering and unprecedented those events, the more need there is for some authoritative schema of interpretation. In the same way that, as J.H. Plumb has remarked in a suitably biblical metaphor, 'the past is the handmaid of authority', so the indivisible act of perception and interpretation of contemporary events relies on some externally imposed or derived system of interpretation. As we have seen, in the early days of the French Revolution it seemed to most Englishmen that such an authoritative schema was offered by the dominant Whig interpretation of the Glorious Revolution of 1688. As the manifest inappropriateness of this specifically English interpretation slowly became apparent, the quest for replacements may be seen also in terms of a quest for alternative kinds of interpretative authority. This does not, as we have seen, necessarily imply any inherent conflict between, say, the natural and biblical metaphors, whether used as a purely secular and psychological shorthand or as revealing direct divine judgement; both trains of imagery had very ancient roots in the mythology and literature of the English-speaking world, as they had in the French. Both may in this sense be seen as historically-sanctioned and therefore politically acceptable systems of interpretation. Burke, like Wordsworth, juxtaposes both sets of imagery without any feeling of incongruity. But, as the debate in England continued through the 1790s and into the 1800s, a latent and essentially subversive ambiguity in both groups of images becomes increasingly apparent.

Olivia Smith has argued in a recent book on the French Revolution debate in England, *The Politics of Language 1791–1819*, that behind the ostensible controversy in England over what was happening in France was another, no less serious, debate over the political control of language itself. In the early stages of the Revolution, she suggests, the radicals and pro-Revolutionary apologists lacked an adequate vocabulary of dissent. To discuss the Revolution at all meant to discuss it in their opponents' terminology. One reason for the massive influence of Burke's *Reflections* on the entire subsequent debate was simply that he had at the outset occupied the linguistic high ground, taking over the language of the Bible and of nature for his case in such a way that anyone who wished to take issue with him was disadvantaged right from the start by being made to appear atheistical, anti-religious and unnatural. Moreover, the powerful rhetorical style of the *Reflections* entrenched its implied claim to be the authoritative and historically-sanctioned interpretation of the Revolution. Many radical pamphleteers of the 1790s were evidently constrained by a feeling that, since they lacked Burke's education and superb command of the language, their 'plain speech' could carry neither the weight nor the implied historical consensus of his judgement.

This is an interesting argument which effectively highlights the often-neglected aspect of the apparent authority bestowed by class and education, especially in the essentially deferential and hierarchical society that was England in the late eighteenth century. But the exceptions are too numerous and powerful for the case to carry total conviction. Tom Paine was certainly not overawed by any feeling of Burke's cultural superiority. Like Cobbett, he had spent sufficient time during his formative years in the newly independent United States of America, where a different kind of egalitarian linguistic idiom was being forged and had learned brilliantly to use the rhetorical power of plain speech. If Burke may be said to have occupied the linguistic high ground of polite society, Paine's apparently artless but highly effective rhetoric managed to make it seem that the *Rights of Man* had a corner in commonsense – and, no less important, that commonsense was the most essential quality in the whole debate. Nor should we ignore the power of Burke's more conventionally educated English opponents. Horne Tooke, Richard Price, Joseph Priestley, William Godwin or Mary Wollstonecraft were none of them culturally overawed by Burke, nor did they seem to have any perceptible difficulty in finding an adequate linguistic idiom in which to debate with him. If the first generation of radical apologists eventually lost the argument with Burke, it was due more to the excesses of the Revolution itself than to any inherent cultural bias in the English language.

Nowhere is this better illustrated than in the cases of the poets Blake, Coleridge and Wordsworth. Though Blake came from a lower social class than the other two and lacked a university education, he was by no means ill-educated. More important, perhaps, in a matter of literary confidence, he did not *feel* at an educational disadvantage. A late eighteenth-century grammar school spent more time on minor Latin authors than major English ones, and contemporary accounts (including those of both Wordsworth and Coleridge) of what Cambridge had to offer in their day do not suggest that its traditional role as a producer of poets had much to do with the formal curriculum. Peacock was not the only writer of our period to regard university education as a complete waste of time. Though, like Peacock, he was self-educated, Blake was never the naive genius or intellectual freak he is sometimes portrayed as being. Through his friendship with Joseph Johnson, the radical London publisher and bookseller, he was during the 1790s a member of a circle that included William Frend (Coleridge's old Cambridge tutor who had been expelled from his Fellowship for his radical politics and Unitarian beliefs), Godwin, Mary Wollstonecraft, Paine, Priestley, Price and Holcroft. Unlike almost any other group in England at this period (and certainly unlike the universities), this largely Unitarian circle was well acquainted with the latest intellectual movements in both France and, what was much rarer, in Germany. Blake's astonishing creation of a personal mythology was firmly rooted not merely in the Bible, but in his reading of the major European classics (including Homer, Virgil and Dante), and we know that by 1803 he was reading Greek and Latin fluently and had begun to learn Hebrew.

Blake's view of the French Revolution is, indeed, in some ways the most purely literary of any of the writers considered here. In part this is a product of the circumstances under which he was working. Unlike the other authors, he was not writing for an established audience, and his poems, which he printed himself, were virtually unknown. Even Coleridge, who was one of the most avid readers of the day, had never come across his poetry until the early 1820s, by which time Blake was over 65. In part, however, this markedly more literary quality is because Blake is less interested in the Revolution as a social and historical phenomenon than as a manifestation of eternal qualities of the human spirit.

Readers of his unfinished poem, *The French Revolution*, the first and only book of which was printed by Johnson in 1791 but never published, are often puzzled to encounter the Duke of Burgundy playing a stirringly patriotic role in the debate at the bankrupt Court of Louis XVI, when it was common knowledge that the last duke of that name had been Louis' elder brother whose early death at the age of 30 had brought the ill-fated younger sibling to the throne. The answer seems to lie in precisely this sense of universal reference that Blake strives to give the local event. According to popular belief, the dead brother had, in Daniel Eaton's words, given 'early presage of excessive pride', and was therefore the perfect symbol of the diehard spirit of the French Crown. Moreover an earlier duke had played a significant patriotic role in the peace negotiations of Shakespeare's *Henry V* – even his celebration of 'our fertile France' finding an echo in Blake's verse. The mixture of myth and topical reference, always such a striking feature of Blake's work, is part of a still fundamentally typological view of history that sees the contemporary world in terms of the greater moral drama of human existence. Hence the French Revolution debate for Blake is essentially prophetic rather than political or social – or rather, the former rightly understood embraces both the latter concerns. In a piece entitled *All Religions are One*, etched in about 1788, Blake's 'Voice of one crying in the Wilderness' had declared:

> The Religions of all Nations are derived from each Nation's different reception of the Poetic Genius, which is every where call'd the Spirit of Prophecy.

It is precisely in this notion of the poet as prophet that the ambiguity inherent in the use of biblical metaphors noted earlier becomes of crucial importance.

The year before this piece, in 1787, there had been published the first full English translation of one of the most influential critical works of the eighteenth century: Robert Lowth's *Lectures on the Sacred Poetry of the Hebrews*. Originally published in Latin in 1745, when Lowth was Professor of Poetry at Oxford, the *Lectures* had inaugurated a critical revolution in both England and Germany. In them Lowth, who was one of the most distinguished biblical scholars of his day (and later to be successively Bishop of St David's, Oxford, and finally, London), had given massive historical support for the aesthetic argument advanced earlier in the century by John Dennis that 'poetry is the natural language of religion'. According to Lowth, the Hebrew word 'Nabi', meant 'a Prophet, a Poet, or a Musician, under the influence of divine inspiration'. In Old Testament times, argued Lowth:

> . . . it is . . . evident, that the prophetic office had a most strict connexion with the poetic art. They had one common name, one common origin, one common author, the Holy Spirit. Those in particular were called to the exercise of the prophetic office, who were previously conversant with the sacred poetry. It was equally part of their duty to compose verses for the service of the church, and to declare the oracles of God.

One of the Hebrew words most commonly used for a poem in the Old Testament ('Mashal') is also the word translated in the New Testament as 'parable'. Rightly understood, the roles of the poet and prophet, according to Lowth, are essentially identical.

The effect of Lowth's scholarly argument on both poetry and biblical studies in the eighteenth century can scarcely be exaggerated. In Germany, where he was swiftly republished with a preface and notes by the leading biblical scholar of the day, Johann David Michaelis, he was one of the major influences on the development of the Higher Criticism and therefore of all modern biblical scholarship. In England, however, it was on the poets that he was to have the greatest impact. From being in Augustan theory the rhetorical embellisher of the great common truths of mankind, the poet, for the Romantics, became the prophetic oracle and discoverer of new truth. It is no accident, for instance, that Burke in his attack in the *Reflections* on Richard Price's eulogy of the French Revolution should have accused Price of being set up as an 'oracle' and of 'chaunting' his 'prophetic song'. Similarly,

Wordsworth's Preface to the *Lyrical Ballads*, often treated nowadays as the manifesto of English Romanticism, is heavily Lowthian in tone.

For Blake the conclusions of Lowth's argument were no less irresistible. The prophetic tradition of Israel had always been marked by a concern with righteousness and social justice, frequently in the form of condemnations of the oppression of the poor by the rich, and the abuse of power by those in authority. This, as Lowth points out, gives a fundamentally different role to Hebrew poetry in comparison with its eighteenth-century European equivalent. Whereas English poetry (like that of the rest of Europe) was the medium of small, mostly university-educated circles, connected either with the Court or with other centres of power and patronage, Hebrew poetry had almost always been the art-form of the opposition: the songs of a rural and pastoral people, bitterly critical of the corruptions of city and Court life.

This biblical sanction for what in effect amounts to political radicalism had corresponding aesthetic consequences. Lowth had singled out for praise the 'simple and unadorned' language of Hebrew verse, which gained what he called its 'almost ineffable sublimity' not by elaborately refined diction or subtlety of metaphor, but by the depth and universality of its subject-matter, expressed in the homely metaphors of agriculture and everyday life. Even when a poet such as David was translated to the Court, he never attempted to conceal that his poetic roots lay still in his early life as a village shepherd boy. Jesus (the descendant of David) by his humble origins and in the simplicity and directness of his language, was similarly continuing in his parables and teaching the Old Testament poetic tradition.

It is in such arguments as these of Lowth that we find, too, the probable origins of the intermingling of natural and supernatural imagery noted earlier in Wordsworth. The closeness to nature of these shepherd and farmer prophets kept them free, Lowth implies, from the more sophisticated temptations of the urban Canaanite society. A retreat to the desert or the wilderness had always been a part of the prophetic training. It is not difficult to see how this biblical withdrawal to nature could be parallelled by Wordsworth's later use of retreat into the Lake District fells, where he retired after the failure of his early revolutionary ideals. Seen in this light it is not difficult to understand the claim made by both Wordsworth and Coleridge in later life that it was not they, but the revolutionaries in France, culminating in that ultimate abomination, Napoleon, who had altered their principles.

Moreover, the critique of conventional Augustan aesthetics implicit in these arguments of Lowth was not missed by his successors. Hugh Blair, one of the most influential critics of Wordsworth's youth and a source of much of the argument for the Preface to the *Lyrical Ballads*, devotes a whole chapter of his *Lectures on Rhetoric and Belles Lettres* (1783) to discussing Lowth's work and its consequences. Similarly, in place of the often stilted diction and imagery of earlier eighteenth-century verse, Lowth's stress on naturalness and simplicity as more 'sublime' anticipates much of Burke's more famous *Enquiry into the Origin of our Ideas of the Sublime and the Beautiful* (1757) by more than a decade and was almost certainly an influence on it. Perhaps even more startling is the way in which Lowth foreshadows the notion, taken up so strongly by both Blair and Wordsworth, that the language of poetry is the product of 'enthusiasm' springing from 'mental emotion'.

Yet if Lowth thus implicitly provided both the argument and supporting evidence for a total revaluation of the literary conventions of his day, it is important to recognise that they had an unimpeachably conservative source. There was nothing radical about the scholarly Oxford professor turned Bishop of London. Yet his work offered the Romantic poets the justification they needed to find in poetry an appropriate medium for social protest and in the language of the Bible and of nature the imagery by which an old and corrupt society might be thrown down and a new and more just order created. It is fascinating here to look at the case of Shelley a generation later, who though he was sent down from Oxford in 1811 for writing the notorious pamphlet, *The Necessity of Atheism*, in both his politically radical poems (such as *The Masque of Anarchy*) and in his aesthetic writings (*The Defence of Poetry*) reverts instinctively to biblical images and phraseology to uphold social justice and the power of poetry. In the new Romantic aesthetics, moreover, were embodied an ideal of plain speech and a return to the language of the people and to subjects of universal concern, that were within a few years of the publication of Blair and the translation of Lowth to play a crucial part in the French Revolution debate. Indeed, it is arguable that, so far from successfully occupying the linguistic high ground by his *Reflections*, Burke is actually fighting a brilliant rearguard action to prevent the language of the Bible and of nature falling automatically to his opponents in the general Romantic shift of sensibilities that he himself had helped to inaugurate with his *Enquiry* over 30 years earlier.

Language, however, does not operate in a vacuum. What turns the scale so decisively in the end and made Burkeians of a kind out of both Wordsworth and Coleridge was not a linguistic or aesthetic debate but the very much more simple, and to them shocking, facts of the execution of the king and queen, the Reign of Terror and the inexorable rise of Napoleon, and with him a gratuitous glorification of militarism worse than anything seen under the *ancien régime*. But that, of course, did not put an end to the much larger underlying debate, which was in a sense only triggered off by the events in France – the debate over the legitimacy of government, the nature of social justice and the attack on institutionalised corruption.

It was inevitable, once the Revolution in France had raised these questions in the minds of thinking people in England, that the subsequent collapse, or at least eclipse, of the revolutionary ideals across the Channel could not put a stop to the political debate in Britain. As we have seen, there was always a sense in which that debate had been one of hermeneutics, concerned less with the state of France than with how the English should interpret those events. Even Burke's *Reflections*, which seem at first sight to be very closely concerned with the actual course of the Revolution, can be seen on closer reading to be concerned with certain more general issues at least as relevant to the British as the French – the nature of change in a society, for instance, and the corresponding need for order. Its full title, we recall, was

Reflections on the Revolution in France, and on the Proceedings in Certain Societies in London Relative to that Event. In a letter intended to have been sent to a gentleman in Paris. Written by an Irishman, it was intended for English consumption, and it is arguable that it successfully laid down the ground-rules for political debate for more than 100 years, not because it was about the French Revolution, but rather because it was *not* primarily about the Revolution so much as general political principles as they applied to a constitutional monarchy such as Britain. When, after the collapse of the English radicals, hopes for the Revolution and the outbreak of war with France, we find the Romantic poets, Wordsworth, Coleridge and Southey, implicitly or explicitly adopting what might be called a 'Burkeian' position, it was not that they came to agree with Burke's views on what had happened in France in 1789–90, but that they came to accept his fundamentally organic view of society. It is here that we encounter the ambiguity in the idea of 'nature' parallelling that we have already discovered in the use of religious imagery.

   For the early eighteenth century, dazzled by the enormous advances in science of the late seventeenth, which in England had centred around the foundation and achievements of the Royal Society and was popularly associated with the name of Newton, the idea of nature carried with it immediate associations of law. On the much publicised analogy with a clock (an image reiterated by successive generations of natural theologians from Leibniz to Paley) the universe was seen as operating according to complex, finely-adjusted, inflexible and totally impersonal mechanical laws, exemplified most strikingly in the laws of gravity and motion postulated by Newton and applied most dramatically to the workings of the solar system and the astronomical universe. A favourite scientific model of the period was the 'orrery', a clockwork model of the solar system showing how the moon and planets revolved both upon their own axes and also around the earth and sun respectively. It was named after Charles Boyle, Earl of Orrery, for whom the first one had been made. A similar idea of nature as a gradually unfolding system of law was celebrated in poetry by Pope in the first book of his *Essay on Man*, which was to become one of the best-known poems of the century.

It was to this view of nature as a vast interlocking mechanism everywhere revealing regularity and order that the original astronomical image of 'revolution' made so strong an initial appeal. There was, so the second book of Pope's *Essay on Man* ingeniously suggested, a direct analogy between God's providential organisation of the macrocosm, the solar system, and the microcosm, man. Just as the universe operated on natural laws that once they were understood could be seen as quite inexorable, so human nature and politics were governed by a similar system of all-powerful natural law. As advanced by Pope this is an essentially conservative doctrine – what Basil Willey has neatly described as 'cosmic Toryism', but it is not difficult to see how such an analogy could be, and eventually was, subverted into an equally compelling doctrine of revolution. David Hartley, for instance, as early as 1749 in his monumental *Observations on Man, his Frame, his Duties, and his Expectations*, had advanced what is called a 'necessitarian' system of psychology. However much human beings might *feel* free, he argued, they were in fact *necessarily* programmed to develop along certain strictly defined paths. While it made no overt references to politics, his system offered what looked like overwhelming scientific evidence for a belief in the perfectibility of man and therefore of society. While there is no evidence that Hartley, who seems to have been guided by strong religious principles, saw his system as being politically radical any more than he did atheistical, it rapidly became clear that his greatest appeal was to radical Unitarian and eventually Utilitarian schools of thought. His *Observations* were republished in an abridged and more secularised version by Priestley, a Unitarian of even more radical necessitarian and perfectionist beliefs, in 1775, and in full, with an engraved frontispiece by Blake, in 1792. So strong was the appeal of Hartley's system to the youthful and radical Unitarian Coleridge in the 1790s that as late as 1798 he named his eldest son after him. Hartley's impact on Bentham, James Mill, and the so-called 'philosophical radicals' was equally strong and more enduring. Finally, shorn of all religious implications, it passed from them to John Stuart Mill to become, in its final manifestation, one of the basic assumptions of Utilitarianism in the mid-nineteenth century. What was to give so many of the radicals and revolutionaries, from Wordsworth to Shelley and Mill to Marx, such confidence in the eventual victory of their cause was the powerful belief that the inexorable laws of 'nature' were on their side.

Yet, though it is important to remember how much Mill, as he was the first to admit, owed to Wordsworth, it would, of course, be over-simple to attribute the same idea of nature to both. The word itself is a notoriously vague one that is capable of bearing many contradictory meanings (see, for instance, my discussion of this in Chapter V of *The Romantics*, [1982], pp.210–11). If, as we have seen, the idea carried overtones not merely of necessity but also of biblical brotherhood, simplicity and what was shared by all men, that had an obvious affinity with the revolutionary slogan of 'Liberty, Equality, and Fraternity', there was another side to the concept that seemed less clear cut – and it was to this that Burke with his brilliant debating instinct had drawn attention. It was a question of mechanism versus organism. To the early part of the eighteenth century it seemed totally appropriate to describe nature primarily as a mechanism, but with the growth of industrialisation (not to mention that of botany and anatomy) it had become clear by the second half of the century that there was a fundamental difference between mechanical and organic structures, and the distinction had become common enough to be used by analogy in literary criticism. Though the former had all the implications of conscious design so beloved of the natural theologians, it also suggested rigidity, inflexibility and lack of powers of adaptation. A machine was no longer a way of modelling the intricate wonders of the solar system, it was a way of repeating identical actions with monotonous and inhuman regularity, as in the Lancashire cotton mill that Wordsworth regards with such horror in *The Excursion*, Book VIII. At intervals machines broke down, or even, as happened all too frequently with the early steam-engines, exploded. When they had served their purpose or could not be repaired, they were scrapped. An organism, in contrast, was more than the sum of its parts.

It was a self-perpetuating part of a continuum that stretched back to the dawn of creation; it was flexible and adaptable to new circumstances. It was active and even (in its human forms) creative rather than passively responding to preset directions. Which of these two models, asks Burke in effect, is the more appropriate analogy for the body politic? The revolution of the machine or the evolution of the organism? Which of these two is the more 'natural'? The former is the one chosen by the French, who have destroyed their political institutions in the belief that reason will enable them to create something altogether new and superior in its place; the latter must be the response of the English, who are historically aware of how delicate and tender a plant is the tree of liberty and how easily it is damaged or destroyed by too sharp a change in its circumstances.

Though Burke was by no means solely responsible for this radical shift of meaning in a stock metaphor, to him must go much of the credit for popularising its political implications. By the early years of the nineteenth century the idea of nature and its associated notions of organism had as clear a heritage in conservative polemic as in radical – indeed, the word 'radical' itself with its semantic implications of getting to the 'root' of the problem presented problems to those who suspected that by digging down to the roots one might be in danger of killing the actual tree. At the very moment, therefore, when defenders of the Revolution in France were invoking the traditional and supposedly 'scientific' idea of nature in its justification, we find that in England where the beginnings of industrialism had given a new and ominously rigid meaning to 'mechanism', the meaning of the word 'nature' itself was undergoing changes making it much less susceptible to revolutionary interpretations. But, of course, there is a distinction between what was then popularly called 'Jacobinism', which was held to favour violent political change on the French model, and the kind of organic change still believed in by most of the English literary radicals. Though neither Bentham nor Mill ever dreamed of advocating revolution in the sense of political violence, their continued implicit assumption that those secularised successors to natural law, the 'sciences' of psychology and economics, would necessarily ensure the eventual triumph of their ideas differentiates them from Wordsworth, whose post-revolutionary ideas of nature contained no such sense of determinism.

Even before this shift in the idea of nature towards the organic and the evolutionary that we associate with Burke and Wordsworth, there had come a much more philosophic onslaught on the traditional Locke-Newton epistemology from Blake. For him the idea of Natural Religion, the very basis of the earlier view of nature, was a complete absurdity. Such arguments from Design for the existence of God, the by-now classical inference of the existence of the 'watchmaker' from the existence of the 'watch', was totally invalid. There is no such thing as a neutral observer, no such thing as perspectiveless knowledge. Our perception of the universe is conditioned by the preconceptions that we bring to it. If to a mechanistic age the mystery of the universe could be reduced to the ingenious cog-wheels of an orrery, that was merely a comment on the prevailing philosophy of the age:

> If it were not for the Poetic or Prophetic character the Philosophic [*i.e. the 'scientific'*] & Experimental would soon be at the ratio of all things, & stand still, unable to do other than repeat the same dull round over again.
>
> *There is No Natural Religion*, 1st Series, Conclusion.

If it were not already clear what Blake intends by 'the same dull round', the point is clarified by what seems to be explicit reference to an orrery in the second series of *There is No Natural Religion*:

> The bounded is loathed by its possessor. The same dull round, even of a universe, would soon become a mill with complicated wheels.
>
> *There is No Natural Religion*, 2nd Series, Proposition IV.

Such passages go far to explain why for Blake the Revolution was less a political than a psychological event. Yet the two were, of course, ultimately inseparable. In *A Vision of the*

Last Judgement (1810) he was to criticise Paine and Voltaire for attempting to live 'in this world' in 'Paradise & Liberty'. 'You cannot have Liberty in this World without what you call Moral Virtue, & you cannot have Moral Virtue without the Slavery of that half of the Human Race who hate what you call Moral Virtue.' The 'freedom' sought by the revolutionaries in France and England alike was by then for Blake a quality to be found in the human spirit rather than political institutions.

And indeed, the later history of the revolutionary debate in England seems to bear out his belief in ways he was unlikely to have suspected. The transformation of images, which, as we have seen, lay at the centre of the polemic, was to affect every level of English society's vision of itself, both for good and ill. At a political level the battle for reform had only just begun in the 1790s, and it was to be waged unremittingly for the next 30 years before a near-revolutionary situation in England finally persuaded a moderate consensus, on good Burkeian principles, to allow the measure of cautious change represented by the 1832 Reform Bill and its attendant legislation. In a number of important respects, however, the terms of the debate, and therefore the images used, remain remarkably constant. The sense of forces at work on a greater than human scale persists and grows, aided by images from that other, metaphorical, revolution of the period, the Industrial Revolution. There is similarly a reiterated contrast between the natural and the unnatural and between apocalyptically conceived religious forces of light and darkness, good and evil. The former imagery is frequent, for instance, in Cobbett; the latter in one of the most prolific radical journalists and publishers of the eighteen-teens, William Hone, whose trial and acquittal in 1817 was a landmark in popular agitation.

With Hone and his fellow popular journalists we find the debate that had begun over liberty and legitimacy in France transformed into one over social conditions and corruption at home. At the same time we also find appearing another kind of imagery which, while it was foreshadowed by Blake and Wordsworth, was to be developed in quite new ways by popular journalism – that of childhood and the unconscious.

In the *Songs of Innocence and of Experience* Blake had, right at the beginning of the Revolution debate, recast the question of freedom versus repression in a series of images of childhood that embraced religious, sexual and natural imagery. Similarly, from his experience of the Revolution Wordsworth, for instance, had by the turn of the century reached an intuitive understanding of the role of what is now called the unconscious in human motivation (*Prelude* (1805), Book XIII) and had, again, insisted on the vital importance of childhood in understanding the adult. Neither, however, had attempted to use the language of childhood in popular satire or to suggest that their opponents were essentially childish. This is precisely what Hone had done in a series of lampoons on the Prince Regent and the Liverpool Administration, using a mixture of religious forms (the catechism, the creeds and the litany) and, even more effectively, children's nursery rhymes, as in *The Political House that Jack Built*. What alarmed the government particularly about Hone was that by using such popular and widely-known forms he was speaking to a quite new mass-audience.

The debate between Burke and Priestley, Godwin, and Wollstonecraft, however radical in tone, had been politically safe in the very simple sense that it was not written for and available to a mass-market. Paine had been much more of a danger and was dealt with correspondingly more severely. But between 1790 and 1810 there had been an enormous increase in literacy. In part this was actually a product of the Revolution debate itself: with such absorbing news from France and excitement at home there was a real incentive for the generation growing up in those years, however humble, to learn to read. Simultaneously there were rapid improvements in printing technology that brought the price of newspapers down to the point where many more families could afford one. Hone's own (unfinished) memoirs record that, when the French National Assembly declared war against Germany, 'My mother began to have, daily, a newspaper, which I read to her and to her sister, who lived with us.'

With changes in printing technology had come, too, the possibility of cheap illustrations. The political cartoon in its modern sense was born, and with Rowlandson, Gillray and

Cruikshank the satirical tradition of Hogarth was available to the new mass-market to support, augment or even replace the reasoned argument and polemic of the earlier period. But if, on the one hand, the new medium had clear connections in visual style with the traditional children's chap-books and similar illustrated juvenile material of the eighteenth century, it was also often brutal, vulgar, indecent and deliberately obscene.

In part this was a direct consequence of the material which was being satirised. The sexual escapades of the portly Prince Regent and the trial of the equally notorious Queen Caroline for adultery were only the most visible antics of an aristocracy whose openly flaunted sex lives were as continual an affront to middle-class morality as its conspicuous wealth was an affront to the starving poor that (literally, in the London of those years) surrounded them. The insatiable appetite of the English public for sexual scandals among its politicians was already well-developed. No doubt the early nineteenth-century aristocrats were, in fact, not significantly more profligate and venial than their ancestors had been: what had changed irrevocably with the Revolution in France was the context. In its aftermath, with the advent of mass-circulation newspapers, the existence of such a class and its right to behave as it wished could, almost for the first time, be called in question by a nascent public opinion. Moreover, in such a context where revolutionary fervour was increasingly matched by evangelical seriousness, it is often difficult to distinguish between old-fashioned licentiousness like that of the Prince Regent and his circle, who behaved much as the aristocracy had always done in the past, and high-principled revolt against conventional morality, as in the case of Mary Wollstonecraft's liaison with Gilbert Imlay in Paris or Shelley's elopement with her daughter, Mary Godwin.

Lady Bessborough is an interesting case in point. She was the witty and talented wife of a prominent politician of the day. She was also a close friend of Charles James Fox and many of his pro-Revolutionary circle. Both she and her sister, Georgiana, Duchess of Devonshire, were also figures of some artistic consequence: one of Georgiana's poems, published in *The Morning Post*, had earned the apparently unironic admiration of Coleridge at a period when he was not in general disposed to admire the aristocracy:

> O Lady, nursed in pomp and pleasure!
> Whence learn'd you that heroic measure?

'Ode to Georgiana', Duchess of Devonshire,
in the 24th stanza in her *Passage over
Mount Gothard*, 1799.

Both sisters, too, had children by their lovers without apparently quarrelling with or parting from their husbands. Lady Bessborough had two children by Lord Granville Leveson Gower, another leading politician, and her sister, the Duchess, one by Charles Grey (later Lord Grey, the Whig prime minister responsible for the 1832 Reform Bill). For some years the Duchess, the Duke, and the Duke's own mistress, Lady Elizabeth Foster, all lived amicably together. Lady Bessborough's (legitimate) daughter, Lady Caroline, married William Lamb, the future Lord Melbourne and Whig prime minister, himself rumoured to be not the child of his putative father, but of Lord Egremont. Caroline was later to distinguish herself by a notorious love-affair with Lord Byron, which she inaugurated by sending him a cutting of her pubic hair in an envelope. Among Lady Bessborough's letters to Lord Gower is a long and quite serious disquisition on the scriptural warrant for Sunday observance and its spiritual value. One of the things that makes it hard for a modern reader to enter into the tone of Regency England is that two very different worlds are overlapping in a way that would have been impossible for the mid-Victorians.

In part, therefore, the virulence and obscenity of many of the new publications reveal revolution in its newly-acquired sense at much deeper levels in the debate. Blake was, as so often, prophetic when in the *Songs of Experience* he related political repression to sexual repression. Many of the millenarian movements that had proliferated in the closing years of the eighteenth century had also been antinomian in their sexual practices; to the pure, it was held, all things were pure, and those thus justified by God could be restricted by neither the laws of Church nor society. Even the Swedenborgians, with whom Blake had been associated for a time, had a schism over whether concubines were permitted in the New Age.

Paulson has argued that the calculated obscenities of Rowlandson express 'in a simpler and less censored form the assumptions about liberty which bordered on rebellion (if not revolution) shared by Sheridan, Fox, and the members of their circle', that is, 'the representation of revolution by pornography'. Many of the leading political revolutionaries in France, Saint-Just, Mirabeau, Camille Desmoulins or Danton, were also openly in revolt against established sexual mores. Saint-Just had seduced a provincial aristocrat's daughter and been forced to flee to Paris where he had written a long pornographic novel. Mirabeau had also written a pornographic novel, *Ma Conversion*, while in prison for eloping with the wife of the Marquis de Monnier. Libertinism was another aspect of the return to nature. This argument has gained unexpected strength with the modern discovery of very concrete evidence to support Burke's contention that the revolutionaries were sexual libertines in a much more organised way than had previously been supposed. The recent work of Iain McCalman has shown that 'a significant number of . . . London bookseller-publishers who had been active infidel-radicals during the post (Napoleonic) war agitation moved into the field of obscene publications.' At a time when it has been claimed that radical agitation was seeking respectability (and therefore wider middle-class support), it turns out that many leading radicals were actually supporting their political activities by profitable pornography businesses (William Hone, incidentally, was not one of them, though it might help to account for his move away from radical agitation in the 1820s). Cobbett himself, however, had to change his publisher, William Benbow, when he discovered what Benbow's staple trade was, but it was useful ammunition to his opponents. A contemporary cartoon (about Canning's wife, Lady Conyngham, who was believed to be having an affair with the Prince Regent) shows the interior of Benbow's shop in the Strand. Among the works advertised are *Sultan Sham and his Seven Wives* (either another attack on the Prince or a piece of pornography or, most likely, both) and *A Peep*

at the Peers, which was in fact a satire on the House of Lords
by Cobbett himself, as well as *Cobbett's Register*.

   Cobbett's clash with his publisher, comic as it may seem
in retrospect, nevertheless expresses a very serious point. The
reformers in England were hardly a homogeneous group.
They ranged from nonconformist clergy such as Richard Price
to commercial pornographers, aristocratic sexual libertines
and occultists such as the members of the notorious 'Hell-
Fire Club', said to include Fox, Sheridan and, with visiting
status, the omnipresent Benjamin Franklin, the American
vice-president, who was not merely creator of the American
Episcopalian Prayer Book but also Grand Master of the Paris
Masonic Lodge of the Nine Sisters, among whose other
members were Franz Anton Mesmer, the inventor of hypnot-
ism, Voltaire, Helvetius and Thomas Jefferson. Richard
Payne Knight, the authority on landscape gardening, was also
the author of *A Discourse on the Worship of Priapus*, published
in a private edition. If for some of these latter figures
political reform also involved overthrowing established sexual
conventions, for Cobbett, a family man, writing for a middle
and upper working-class readership, it most definitely did
not. We cannot begin to understand the complexity or far-
reaching nature of the French Revolution debate and the
fears, both conscious and unconscious, that it aroused unless
we see how the reactions to the Revolution came to permeate
the whole of English life. If we try to separate the original
debate over the French Revolution in the early 1790s from
the later radical agitation over reform in England, we distort
what was essentially a continuing controversy that was to
involve every level of perception from questions of public
order and governmental legitimacy to aesthetics, language,
religious belief and sexual mores. So far from proceeding in
an ordered circle to return to its starting-point, in a very real
sense the Revolution had turned the world not merely upside
down but inside out, challenging both society and the psyche.

2 A Mirror for 1688: Refractions and Reflections

Richard Price

The connection between the events in France of 1788–89 and the English Revolution of 1688 was given immediate and powerful rhetorical sanction by Richard Price (1723–91), a leading nonconformist minister of the day who, on 4 November 1789, delivered a *Discourse on the Love of Our Country* at the Meeting House in the Old Jewry (a street in London) to the Society for Commemorating the Revolution in Great Britain.

An almost exact contemporary of Burke's, Price had also made a name for himself as a young man as a philosopher: his *Review of the Principal Questions of Morals* had been published in 1756 (the year before Burke's *Enquiry into the Sublime and the Beautiful*). Like Burke, moreover, Price was not an Englishman by origin, and his Welsh nonconformist background gave him a particular critical stance towards the London society where he passed most of his adult life as a minister first at Newington and then at Hackney in the north-east London suburbs. He was also an able mathematician and economist (among other things an expert on insurance) and had advised several Whig administrations on fiscal reform. Politically he is best described as a moderate radical. His support for the Colonists during the American War of Independence had led to a close friendship with Benjamin Franklin and even to an invitation from the American Congress to emigrate and take up residence there – something which both Paine and Priestley were later to do. Price was also a member of the radical circle centring on the house of Joseph Johnson, which included Godwin, Mary Wollstonecraft, Paine, Priestley, Holcroft and Blake.

Originally Price had been invited to give the commemorative sermon at the Presbyterian chapel in Old Jewry the year before, on the 100th anniversary of the 1688 Revolution. During the intervening year the Bastille had fallen in France, and there had been renewed agitation in England for the repeal of the Test Acts, which effectively barred Dissenters from the universities and from public life in general.

Price's sermon is a rhetorical masterpiece and one of the classic statements of what was to become known in the nineteenth century as 'liberalism'. He sees the French ideals of *liberté*, *egalité* and *fraternité* in terms of his own deeply-held belief in the peaceful evolution of human society under conditions of personal liberty, democracy and freedom of speech, which were the true goals of the 1688 English revolution but which had so far been best fulfilled by the emerging American democracy.

He begins with a deliberately uncontroversial definition of patriotism in moral terms:

> . . . By our country is meant, in this case, not the soil or the spot of earth on which we happen to have been born; not the forests and fields, but that community of which we are members; or that body of companions and friends and kindred who are associated with us under the same constitution of government, protected by the same laws, and bound together by the same civil polity.
>
> . . . It is proper to observe, that even in this sense of our country, that love of it which is our duty, does not imply any conviction of the superior value of it to other countries, or any particular preference of its laws and constitution of government. Were this implied, the love of their country would be the duty of only a very small part of mankind; for there are few countries that enjoy the advantage of laws and governments which deserve to be preferred. To found, therefore, this duty on such a preference, would be to found it on error and delusion. It is, however, a common delusion. There is the same partiality in countries, to themselves, that there is in individuals. All our attachments should be accompanied, as far as possible,

with right opinions. – We are too apt to confine wisdom and virtue within the circle of our own acquaintance and party. Our friends, our country, and in short every thing related to us, we are disposed to overvalue. A wise man will guard himself against this delusion. He will study to think of all things as they are, and not suffer any partial affections to blind his understanding. In other families there may be as much worth as our own. In other circles of friends there may be as much wisdom; and in other countries as much of all that deserves esteem; but, notwithstanding this, our obligation to love our own families, friends, and country, and to seek, in the first place, their good, will remain the same. . . .

A Discourse on the Love of Our Country (1789), pp.2–4.

This innate affection for our families, friends and nation, he argues, must not make us blind to the faults of our own society nor to the virtues of those different from our own. Price will have nothing to do with the kind of cheap unthinking jingoism that says 'My country, right or wrong'. For him patriotism involves not merely a love of one's country but a corresponding recognition of similar sentiments in others:

I . . . desire you particularly to distinguish between the love of our country and that spirit of rivalship and ambition which has been common among nations. – What has the love of their country hitherto been among mankind? What has it been but a love of domination; a desire of conquest, and a thirst for grandeur and glory, by extending the territory, and enslaving surrounding countries? What has it been but a blind and narrow principle, producing in every country a contempt of other countries, and forming men into combinations and factions against their common rights and liberties? This is the principle that has been too often cried up as a virtue of the first rank: a principle of the same kind with that which governs clans of *Indians* or tribes of *Arabs*, and leads them out to plunder and massacre. As most of the evils which have taken place in private life, and among individuals, have been occasioned by the desire of private interest overcoming the public affections; so most of the evils which have taken place among bodies of men have been occasioned by the desire of their own interest overcoming the principle of universal benevolence: and leading them to attack one another's territories, to encroach on one another's rights, and to endeavour to build their own advancement on the degradation of all within reach of their power. . . .

I must desire you to recollect that we are so constituted that our affections are more drawn to some among mankind than to others, in proportion to their degrees of nearness to us, and our power of being useful to them. It is obvious that this is a circumstance in the constitution of our natures which proves the wisdom and goodness of our Maker; for had our affections been determined alike to all our fellow-creatures, human life would have been a scene of embarrassment and distraction. Our regards, according to the order of nature, begin with ourselves; and every man is charged primarily with the care of himself. Next come our families, and benefactors, and friends; and after them our country. We can do little for the interest of mankind at large. To this interest, however, all other interests are subordinate. The noblest principle in our nature is the regard to general justice, and that good-will which embraces all the world. – I have already observed this; but it cannot be too often repeated. Though our immediate attention must be employed in promoting our own interest and that of our nearest connexions; yet we must remember, that a narrower interest ought always to give way to a more extensive interest. In pursuing particularly the interest of our country, we ought to carry our views beyond it. We should love it ardently, but not exclusively. We ought to seek its good, by all the means that our different circumstances and abilities will allow; but at the same time we ought to consider ourselves as citizens of the world, and take care to maintain a just regard to the rights of other countries.

                                              Ibid., pp.4–10.

Price believes in the powers of religion, education and free speech to enlighten humanity and develop its powers to the level where it will be fit for self-government. For him it is axiomatic that religion and democracy go hand-in-hand. If men are equal before God, it follows that they are also equal before the law and are thus entitled, as of right, to an equal share in determining their own fate:

> Our first concern, as lovers of our country, must be to *enlighten* it. – Why are the nations of the world so patient under despotism? – Why do they crouch to tyrants, and submit to be treated as if they were a herd of cattle? Is it not because they are kept in darkness, and want knowledge? Enlighten them and you will elevate them. Shew them they are *men*, and they will act like *men*. Give them just ideas of civil government, and let them know that it is an expedient for gaining protection against injury and defending their rights, and it will be impossible for them to submit to governments which, like most of those now in the world, are usurpations on the rights of men, and little better than contrivances for enabling the *few* to oppress the *many*. Convince them that the Deity is a righteous and benevolent as well as omnipotent being, who regards with equal eye all his creatures, and connects his favour with nothing but an honest desire to know and do his will; and that zeal for mystical doctrines which has led men to hate and harass one another will be exterminated. Set religion before them as a rational service, consisting not in any rites and ceremonies, but in worshipping God with a pure heart and practising righteousness from the fear of his displeasure and the apprehension of a future righteous judgment, and that

gloomy and cruel superstition will be abolished which has hitherto gone under the name of religion, and to the support of which civil government has been perverted. – Ignorance is the parent of bigotry, intolerance, persecution and slavery. Inform and instruct mankind, and these evils will be excluded. – Happy is the person who, himself raised above vulgar errors, is conscious of having aimed at giving mankind this instruction. Happy is the Scholar or Philosopher who at the close of life can reflect that he has made this use of his learning and abilities: but happier far must he be, if at the same time he has reason to believe he has been successful, and actually contributed, by his instructions, to disseminate among his fellow creatures just notions of themselves, of their rights, of religion, and the nature and end of civil government.

Ibid., pp.11–14.

Though some might feel that his use of 'men' to cover the whole human race was sexist in today's terminology, Price's general position is one that, by and large, has become a twentieth-century norm, and it is difficult for the modern reader to grasp how radical the implications of his argument would have been to conservative eighteenth-century people. Such a discussion of 'rights' was uncontroversial only in so far as it could be couched in terms general enough to suggest that the oppression of the many by the few was something that happened elsewhere in the world – specifically, he suggests by his examples, among such safely far-away peoples as the Spaniards, Turks and Russians. Now, however, he turns to draw direct parallels between the traditional heroes of English liberty from the seventeenth-century Civil War and the French eighteenth-century Enlightenment figures whom he sees as standing in a similar relation to the Revolution now in progress:

Such were *Milton, Locke, Sidney, Hoadly*, etc. in this country; such were *Montesquieu, Marmontel, Turgot*, etc. in France. They sowed a seed which has since taken root, and is now growing up to a glorious harvest. To the information they conveyed by their writings we owe those revolutions in which every friend to mankind is now exulting. – What an encouragement is this to us all in our endeavours to enlighten the world? Every degree of illumination which we can communicate must do the greatest good. It helps to prepare the minds of men for the recovery of their rights, and hastens the overthrow of priestcraft and tyranny. – In short, we may, in this instance, learn our duty from the conduct of the oppressors of this world. They know that light is hostile to them, and therefore they labour to keep men in the dark. With this intention they have appointed licensers of the press; and, in Popish countries, prohibited reading of the Bible. Remove the darkness in which they envelope the world, and their usurpations will be exposed, their power will be subverted, and the world emancipated.

Ibid., pp.14–15.

Holding fast to the principles of the Glorious Revolution Price goes on to spell out the implications of constitutional monarchy that he sees as enshrined in the 1688 settlement. Though he has been careful to prepare his ground by starting with first principles so unexceptionable that even his most Tory opponents could hardly have disagreed, each step of the argument is bringing him on to more and more controversial territory. The description that follows of the position of King George III – a simple obstinate man, known popularly as 'Farmer George' – is a brilliant piece of radical polemic, professing to accept the conventional hyperbole and rhetoric of Parliament and Prayer-Book, while giving it an explanatory gloss of an unambiguously democratic nature:

Civil governors are properly the servants of the public; and a King is no more than the first servant of the public, created by it, maintained by it, and responsible to it: and to all homage paid him, is due to him on no other account than his relation to the public. His sacredness is the sacredness of the community. His authority is the authority of the community; and the term MAJESTY, which it is usual to apply to him, is by no means *his own* majesty, but the MAJESTY OF THE PEOPLE. For this reason, whatever he may be in his private capacity; and though, in respect of personal qualities, not equal to, or even far below many among ourselves – For this reason, I say, (that is, as representing the community and its first magistrate): he is entitled to our reverence and obedience. The words MOST EXCELLENT MAJESTY are rightly applied to him: and there is a respect which it would be criminal to withhold from him.

You cannot be too attentive to this observation. The improvement of the world depends on the attention to it: nor will mankind be ever as virtuous and happy, as they are capable of being, till the attention to it becomes universal and efficacious. If we forget it, we shall be in danger of an idolatry as gross and stupid as that of the ancient heathens, who, after fabricating blocks of wood or stone, fell down and worshipped them.

Ibid., pp.23–24.

. . . Let us . . . take care not to forget the principles of the Revolution. This Society has, very properly, in its Reports, held out these principles, as an instruction to the public. I will only take notice of the three following:

First; The right to liberty of conscience in religious matters.

Secondly; The right to resist power when abused. And,

Thirdly; The right to chuse our own governors; to cashier them for misconduct; and to frame a government for ourselves.

On these three principles, and more especially the last, was the Revolution founded. Were it not true that liberty of conscience is a sacred right; that power abused justifies resistance; and that civil authority is a delegation from the people – Were not, I say, all this true; the Revolution would have been not an ASSERTION, but an INVASION of rights; not a REVOLUTION, but a REBELLION. Cherish in your breasts this conviction, and act under its influence; detesting the odious doctrines of passive obedience, non-resistance, and the divine right of kings – doctrines which, had they been acted upon in this country, would have left us at this time wretched slaves – doctrines which imply, that God made mankind to be oppressed and plundered; and which are no less a blasphemy against him, than an insult on common sense.

I would farther direct you to remember, that though the Revolution was a great work, it was by no means a perfect work; and that all was not then gained which was necessary to put the kingdom in the secure and complete possession of the blessings of liberty. – In particular, you should recollect, that the toleration then obtained was imperfect. It included only those who could declare their faith in the doctrinal articles of the church of England. It has, indeed, been since extended, but not sufficiently; for there still exist penal laws on account of religious opinions, which (were they carried into execution) would shut up many of our places of worship, and silence and imprison some of our ablest and best men.

Ibid., pp.34–36.

Once again, Price disingenuously reminds us, he is doing no more than spell out the fundamental implications of the 1688 Revolution – a word still used by him here explicitly in its old sense and for which the Society for Commemorating the Revolution has always stood. The advent of the Revolution in France, he implies, must recall the British to the unfinished nature of their own revolution: the civil liberties implicit in that have not yet been achieved, and so corruption has been enabled to flourish in the public life. As a nonconformist Price himself had been denied the right to vote, and, not surprisingly, this is a matter for him of some bitterness:

> But the most important instance of the imperfect state in which the Revolution left our constitution, is the INEQUALITY OF OUR REPRESENTATION. I think, indeed, this defect in our constitution so gross and so palpable, as to make it excellent chiefly in form and theory. You should remember that a representation in the legislature of a kingdom is the *basis* of constitutional liberty in it; and that without it a government is nothing but an usurpation. When the representation is fair and equal, and at the same time vested with such powers as our House of Commons possesses, a kingdom may be said to govern itself, and consequently to possess true liberty. When the representation is partial, a kingdom possesses liberty only partially; and if extremely partial, it only gives a *semblance* of liberty; but if not only extremely partial, but corruptly chosen, and under corrupt influence after being chosen, it becomes a *nuisance*, and produces the worst of all forms of government – a government by corruption – a government carried on and supported by spreading venality and profligacy through a kingdom. . . .
>
> The inadequateness of our representation has been long a subject of complaint. This is, in truth, our fundamental grievance; and I do not think that any thing is much more our duty, as men who love their country, and are grateful for the Revolution, than to unite our zeal in endeavouring to get it redressed. At the time of the American war, associations were formed for this purpose in LONDON, and other parts of the kingdom; and our present Minister himself has, since that war, directed to it an effort which made him a favourite with many of us. But all attention to it seems now lost, and the probability is, that this inattention will continue, and that nothing will be done towards gaining for us this essential blessing, till some great calamity again alarms our fears, or till some great abuse

of power again provokes our resentment; or, perhaps, till the acquisition of a pure and equal representation by other countries (while we are mocked with the shadow) kindles our shame.

Ibid., pp.39–42.

In his concluding peroration Price at last releases all the pent-up emotion of his nature. Like Wordsworth, he believes that with the American and now the French Revolution, a new dawn for mankind is breaking and that his own country cannot but follow in the general movement towards liberty and democracy that is spreading inexorably across the face of the earth.

> What an eventful period this is! I am thankful that I have lived to it; and I could almost say, *Lord, now lettest thou thy servant depart in peace, for mine eyes have seen thy salvation.* I have lived to see a diffusion of knowledge, which has undermined superstition and error – I have lived to see the rights of men better understood than ever; and nations panting for liberty, which seemed to have lost the idea of it. – I have lived to see THIRTY MILLIONS of people, indignant and resolute, spurning at slavery, and demanding liberty with an irresistible voice; their king led in triumph, and an arbitrary monarch surrendering himself to his subjects. – After sharing in the benefits of one Revolution, I have been spared to be a witness to two other Revolutions, both glorious. – And now, methinks, I see the ardor for liberty catching and spreading; a general amendment beginning in human affairs; the dominion of kings changed for the dominion of laws, and the dominion of priests giving way to the dominion of reason and conscience.
>
> Be encouraged, all ye friends of freedom, and writers in its defence! The times are auspicious. Your labours have not been in vain. Behold kingdoms, admonished by you, starting from sleep, breaking their fetters, and claiming justice from their oppressors! Behold, the

light you have struck out, after setting AMERICA
free, reflected to FRANCE, and there kindled into a
blaze that lays despotism in ashes, and warms and
illuminates EUROPE!

Tremble all ye oppressors of the world! Take warning all ye supporters of slavish governments, and slavish
hierarchies! Call no more (absurdly and wickedly)
REFORMATION, innovation. You cannot hold the
world in darkness. Struggle no longer against increasing
light and liberality. Restore to mankind their rights;
and consent to the correction of abuses, before they
and you are destroyed together.

Ibid., pp.49–51.

Edmund Burke

Burke's *Reflections* are a direct attack upon Price's sermon –
as he makes clear in his preamble.

Edmund Burke (1729–97) though an Anglican – as he had
to be under the Test Acts to hold a seat in Parliament – was
not merely Irish, but of Catholic background, and it may be
his greater understanding of that troubled country that gave
him a stronger sense than many of his English contemporaries
of the chaos and tyranny that lay ahead in France. Part of
the immense prestige that the *Reflections* were to gain over
the years immediately succeeding their publication in 1790
was due to their uncanny predictions of the course of the
Revolution towards regicide, terror and military dictatorship;
part, too, is due to the sheer rhetorical power of the writing;
but as important as either of these in the long run is the way
in which they were to set the agenda for political debate for
at least a generation.

There is a very real paradox here that contemporaries
themselves were not blind to. Burke – the outsider, the Irish
parvenu – poses as the archetypal conservative and champion
of the monarchy, the aristocracy and a society based upon
hierarchy and deference. Yet at the same time his stance is
sharply anti-metaphysical: some of his strongest irony is

reserved for the 'true religion' of Price's biblical interpretation of the French Revolution. Burke's 'conservatism' is, in fact, not conservative at all in the sense that many of his contemporaries would understand it. The *status quo* that he wishes to preserve is not that of the Divine Right of Kings, but the essentially bourgeois social contract established by the 1688 Revolution. He recognises that the French Revolution, like the earlier English one, is primarily middle-class in character, but also sees that the French version, in attempting to sweep away the entire social underpinning of the old order had rendered itself unstable, and liable to be overthrown in turn by more violent forces until force itself, rather than law, becomes the ultimate sanction – a prophecy aptly fulfilled by Napoleon. Instead, he advances the relatively new and in many ways 'Romantic' view of society as an organism whose parts are subordinate to the 'life' of the whole – an argument that was to have a profound influence upon writers as dissimilar as Coleridge, Disraeli and Newman. Stemming from this basic model are a number of other features that were to become common currency in Romantic thought within a few years: a deep suspicion of abstract systems and logic – especially when applied to human affairs – and, in place of the Enlightenment 'internationalism' reflected by Price, who was careful to define 'country' purely in terms of community rather than 'forests and fields', a corresponding elevation of the importance of family, specific geographical locality and country.

The *Reflections* were rapidly translated into French by Pierre-Gaeton Dupont and into German by Friedrich von Gentz, and in both countries figure significantly in the ensuing ideological debates.

They take the form of a 'letter' to an unnamed 'gentleman in Paris' who has evidently been reading Price's Sermon and has apparently been enquiring as to the status of both his Society and another, similar body, called the Constitutional Society:

> I certainly have the honour to belong to more clubs than one, in which the constitution of this kingdom and the principles of the glorious Revolution, are held

in high reverence: and I reckon myself among the most forward in my zeal for maintaining that constitution and those principles in their utmost purity and vigour. It is because I do so, that I think it necessary for me, that there should be no mistake. Those who cultivate the memory of our revolution, and those who are attached to the constitution of this kingdom, will take good care how they are involved with persons who, under the pretext of zeal towards the Revolution and Constitution, too frequently wander from their true principles; and are ready on every occasion to depart from the firm but cautious and deliberate spirit which produced the one, and which presides in the other.

Reflections on the Revolution in France (1790),
7th edn, p.2.

'I am not,' he adds with rhetorical indignation, 'and . . . I have never been, a member of either of these societies.' The Constitutional Society he dismisses as a recent organisation which is basically little more than a book club; towards what he calls by tactical abbreviation the 'Revolution Society', the society to which Price belonged, he is much more scathing:

Since you have selected the Revolution Society as the great object of your national thanks and praises, you will think me excuseable in making its late conduct the subject of my observations. The National Assembly of France has given importance to these gentlemen by adopting them; and they return the favour, by acting as a committee in England for extending the principles of the National Assembly. Henceforward we must consider them as a kind of privileged persons; as no inconsiderable members in the diplomatic body. This is one among the revolutions which have given splendour to obscurity, and distinction to undiscerned merit. Until very lately I do not recollect to have heard of this club. I am quite sure that it never occupied a moment of my thoughts; nor, I believe, those of any person out of their own set. I find, upon enquiry, that on the anniversary of the Revolution in 1688, a club of dissenters, but of what denomination I know not, have long had the custom of hearing a sermon in one of their churches; and that afterwards they spent the day cheerfully, as other clubs do, at the tavern. But I never heard that any public measure, or political system, much less than the merits of the constitution of any foreign nation, had been the subject of a formal proceeding at their festivals; until, to my inexpressible surprize, I found them in a sort of public capacity, by a congratulatory address, giving an authoritative sanction to the proceedings of the National Assembly in France.

Ibid., pp.4–5.

All this is by way of a preamble to his main attack which is not so much on the Revolution Society as on the main thrust of Price's Sermon itself – and, in particular, on what he sees (correctly as it turned out) as the weakest point in Price's case: that the English Revolution of 1688, the American Revolution and the French Revolution are all essentially manifestations of the same spirit. Wisely, perhaps, Burke does not discuss the Americans. What is happening in France, however, he declares, gives him 'a considerable degree of uneasiness':

The beginnings of confusion with us in England are at present feeble enough; but with you, we have seen an infancy still more feeble, growing by moments into a strength to heap mountains upon mountains, and to wage war with Heaven itself. Whenever our neighbour's house is on fire, it cannot be amiss for the engines to play a little on our own.

Ibid., pp.10–11.

Burke's main concern, he insists, is with his own country. But, as Price has demonstrated, what view we take of events in France will have an immediate bearing on the situation in England. Something very dangerous is afoot and it is for

Burke the more dangerous because of the views of men like Price who are unable to distinguish between things that differ quite fundamentally. So far from being a rerun of the 1688 English Revolution, what is happening in France is something altogether unprecedented in human history:

> It looks to me as if I were in a great crisis, not of the affairs of France alone, but of all Europe, perhaps of more than Europe. All circumstances taken together, the French Revolution is the most astonishing that has hitherto happened in the world. The most wonderful things are brought about in many instances by means the most absurd and ridiculous; in the most ridiculous modes; and apparently, by the most contemptible instruments. Every thing seems out of nature in this strange chaos of levity and ferocity, and of all sorts of crimes jumbled together with all sorts of follies. In viewing this monstrous tragi-comic scene, the most opposite passions necessarily succeed, and sometimes mix with each other in the mind; alternate contempt and indignation; alternate laughter and tears; alternate scorn and horror.
>
> Ibid., pp.11–12.

Price is in all probability an honourable and virtuous man – Burke here plays the role of a somewhat patronising and condescending Mark Antony towards a marginal and dissenting Brutus, but he is dangerous because he is the tool of much more sinister political interests: 'literary caballers', 'intriguing philosophers', 'political theologians and theological politicians', who have 'set him up as a sort of oracle; because, with the best intentions in the world . . . [he] chaunts his prophetic song in exact unison with their designs.' The ironic use of Lowth at this point also highlights a paradoxical and even puzzling quality of Burke's own position here. The Irish parvenu who had spent by far the greater part of his political career in the wilderness is now writing as the self-appointed spokesman for the political establishment and, as if to proclaim his assimilation, he has apparently adopted an anti-intellectual-

ism that comes oddly from a man who earlier in his career
had written one of the most successful books of aesthetics of
the century. Yet to assume, as many of his opponents did,
that Burke is simply a hypocrite who has seen an opportunity
to sell himself to the establishment is hardly adequate. It is
rather that Burke is an intellectual whose political theory
provides excellent theoretical grounds for mistrusting the role
of political theory in politics, especially when it leans towards
too rapid or radical change. He therefore begins his argument
by disputing the theoretical base of Price's argument on
historical grounds:

> There is ground enough for the opinion that all the
> kingdoms of Europe were, at a remote period, elective,
> with more or fewer limitations in the objects of choice;
> but whatever kings might have been here or elsewhere,
> a thousand years ago, or in whatever manner the ruling
> dynasties of England or France may have begun, the
> King of Great Britain is at this day king by a fixed
> rule of succession, according to the laws of his country;
> and whilst the legal conditions of the compact of
> sovereignty are performed by him (as they are per-
> formed) he holds his crown in contempt of the choice
> of the Revolution Society, who have not a single vote for
> a king amongst them, either individually or collectively;
> though I make no doubt they would soon erect
> themselves into an electoral college, if things were ripe
> to give effect to their claim. His majesty's heirs and
> successors, each in his time and order, will come to
> the crown with the same contempt of their choice with
> which his majesty has succeeded to that he wears.
>   Whatever may be the success of evasion in explaining
> away the gross error of *fact*, which supposes that his
> majesty (though he holds it in concurrence with the
> wishes) owes his crown to the choice of his people,
> yet nothing can evade their full explicit declaration,
> concerning the principle of a right in the people
> to choose, which right is directly maintained, and
> tenaciously adhered to. All the oblique insinuations
> concerning election bottom in this proposition, and

are referable to it. Lest the foundation of the king's exclusive legal title should pass for a mere rant of adulatory freedom, the political Divine proceeds dogmatically to assert, that by the principle of the Revolution the people of England have acquired three fundamental rights, all which, with him, compose one system and lie together in one short sentence; namely, that we have acquired a right

1. 'To choose our own governors.'
2. 'To cashier them for misconduct.'
3. 'To frame a government for ourselves.'

This new and hitherto unheard-of bill of rights, though made in the name of the whole people, belongs to those gentlemen and their faction only. The body of the people of England have no share in it. They utterly disclaim it. They will resist the practical assertion of it with their lives and fortunes. They are bound to do so by the laws of their country, made at the time of that very Revolution, which is appealed to in favour of the fictitious rights claimed by the society which abuses its name.

Ibid., pp.19–21.

The fact is, declares Burke, the analogy between the 1688 Revolution and what is now happening in France is fundamentally misconceived. Though this is, of course, the central argument of his whole book, because that case is concerned with the nature of law, he is careful to present it here in narrowly legalistic terms. The 'principles' of the English Revolution are those laid down by legal statute – neither more nor less. Other interpretations are simply those of inexperienced 'enthusiasts' (a word we shall have more to say about in a later section). Thus even the gratuitous pun between 'jury' and 'jewry' is, in that sense, part of the overall structure of his case:

These gentlemen of the Old Jewry, in all their reasonings on the Revolution of 1688, have a revolution which happened in England about forty years before, and the late French revolution, so much before their eyes, and in their hearts, that they are constantly confounding all the three together. It is necessary that we should separate what they confound. We must recall their erring fancies to the *acts* of the Revolution which we revere, for the discovery of its true *principles*. If the *principles* of the Revolution of 1688 are any where to be found, it is in the statute called the *Declaration of Right*. In that most wise, sober, and considerate declaration, drawn up by great lawyers and great statesmen, and not by warm and inexperienced enthusiasts, not one word is said, nor one suggestion made, of a general right 'to choose our own *governors*; to cashier them for misconduct; and to *form* a government for *ourselves*'.

Ibid., p.21.

The legalistic tone to Burke's argument is an important part of his strategy. Freedom is not so much a right in any abstract sense that is a necessary part of being human, but an *inheritance* that is handed down to the British people as any piece of property might be. Indeed, it is rapidly clear that Burke's definition of 'liberty' is conceived more in terms of safeguards to the inheritance of property than in the right to vote. In this he is in line with the assumptions of many of his parliamentary colleagues who would have felt that only those with what was called 'a stake in the country' (i.e. a substantial amount of property) should be called upon to govern.

Yet, of course, the metaphor has some curious and, I suspect, entirely intentional implications. Though he does not say so, we must suppose that those who, like the unfortunate French, do not have any such bequest of liberty made to them by their ancestors have no right to expect it. This is such a startlingly illiberal doctrine as to give us pause. Yet the clue to his meaning here lies, I think, in what follows. Burke's strategy is to ground the rule of law in something much more basic and universal than the precise wording of any particular statutes: Nature itself. 'By a constitutional policy, working after the pattern of nature, we receive, we hold, we transmit our government and our privileges, in the same manner in which we enjoy and transmit our property and our lives.' As we have seen earlier, this represents nothing less than a brilliant attempt to reclaim from the revolutionaries the metaphors and rhetoric of nature, while at the same time insisting on the traditional connections between the idea of nature and that of law. At the same time Burke shows himself prophetically aware of a phenomenon which has uncomfortably dogged almost every twentieth-century attempt to transplant Westminster-style democracy to countries which lack the predominantly Anglo-Saxon culture out of which it grew historically: namely, that it seems almost impossible to create by fiat instant democratic liberties in societies that have not possessed them historically. The twentieth-century military dictatorships of Africa, Asia, South America, and even Europe illustrate in melancholy and repetitive detail that whether or not Burke's metaphor of liberty as an inherited property is justified, the phenomenon it describes is real enough – and much of the subsequent prestige of the *Reflections* was based on the speedy fulfilment of his prophecy of what was to follow in France:

> You will observe, that from Magna Charta to the Declaration of Right, it has been the uniform policy of our constitution to claim and assert our liberties, as an *entailed inheritance* derived to us from our forefathers, and to be transmitted to our posterity; as an estate specially belonging to the people of this kingdom without any reference whatever to any other more general or prior right. By this means our constitution preserves an unity in so great a diversity of its parts. We have an inheritable crown; and inheritable peerage; and an house of commons and a people inheriting privileges, franchises, and liberties, from a long line of ancestors.
> This policy appears to me to be the result of profound reflection; or rather the happy effect of following nature, which is wisdom without reflection,

and above it. A spirit of innovation is generally the result of a selfish temper and confined views. People will not look forward to posterity, who never look backward to their ancestors. Besides, the people of England well know, that the ideal of inheritance furnishes a sure principle of conservation, and a sure principle of transmission; without that all excluding a principle of improvement. It leaves acquisition free; but it secures what it acquires. Whatever advantages are obtained by a state proceeding on these maxims, are locked fast as in a sort of family settlement; grasped as in a kind of mort-main for ever. By a constitutional policy, working after the pattern of nature, we receive, we hold, we transmit our government and our privileges, in the same manner in which we enjoy and transmit our property and our lives. The institutions of policy, the goods of fortune, the gifts of Providence, are handed down, to us and from us, in the same course and order. Our political system is placed in a just correspondence and symmetry with the order of the world, and with the mode of existence decreed to a permanent body composed of transitory parts; wherein, by the disposition of a stupendous wisdom, moulding together the great mysterious incorporation of the human race, the whole, at one time, is never old, or middle-aged, or young, but in a condition of unchangeable constancy, moves on through the varied tenour of perpetual decay, fall, renovation, and progression. Thus, by preserving the method of nature in the conduct of the state, in what we improve we are never wholly new; in what we retain we are never wholly obsolete. By adhering in this manner and on those principles to our forefathers, we are guided not by the superstition of antiquarians, but by the spirit of philosophic analogy. In this choice of inheritance we have given to our frame of polity the image of a relation in blood; binding up the constitution of our country with our dearest domestic ties; adopting our fundamental laws into the bosom of our family affections; keeping inseparable, and cherishing with the warmth of all their combined and mutually reflected charities, our state, our hearths, our sepulchres, and our altars.

Through the same plan of a conformity to nature in our artificial institutions, and by calling in the aid of her unerring and powerful instincts, to fortify the fallible and feeble contrivances of our reason, we have derived several other, and those of no small benefits, from considering our liberties in the light of an inheritance. Always acting as if in the presence of canonized fore-fathers, the spirit of freedom, leading in itself to misrule and excess, is tempered with an awful gravity. This idea of a liberal descent inspires us with a sense of habitual native dignity, which prevents that upstart insolence almost inevitably adhering to and disgracing those who are the first acquirers of any distinction. By this means our liberty becomes a noble freedom. It carries an imposing and majestic aspect. It has a pedigree and illustrating ancestors. It has its bearings and its ensigns armorial. It has a gallery of portraits; its monumental inscriptions; its records, evidences, and titles. We procure reverence to our civil institutions on the principle upon which nature teaches us to revere individual men; on account of their age; and on account of those from whom they are descended. All your sophisters cannot produce any thing better adapted to preserve a rational and manly freedom than the course that we have pursued, who have chosen our nature rather than our speculations, our breasts rather than our inventions, for the great conservatories and maga-zines of our rights and privileges.

Ibid., pp.47–50.

This is Burke at his most rhetorically brilliant, and the experience of two centuries has done little to lessen the controversial force of this argument. Yet he is at pains to dispel the idea that he wishes simply to preserve the *status quo* or to keep government simply as the preserve of a particular class or coterie – however much it might prove to be so in practice:

You do not imagine, that I wish to confine power, authority, and distinction to blood, and names, and titles. No, Sir. There is no qualification for government, but virtue and wisdom, actual or pre-sumptive. Wherever they are actually found, they have, in whatever state, condition, profession or trade, the passport of Heaven to human place and honour. Woe to the country which would madly and impiously reject the service of the talents and virtues, civil, military, or religious, that are given to grace and to serve it; and would condemn to obscurity every thing formed to diffuse lustre and glory around a state. Woe to that country too, that passing into the opposite extreme, considers a low education, a mean contracted view of things, a sordid mercenary occupation, as a preferable title to command. Every thing ought to be open; but not indifferently to every man. No rotation; no appointment by lot; no mode of election operating in the spirit of sortition or rotation, can be generally good in a government conversant in extensive objects.

Ibid., pp.73–74.

Above all, Burke is concerned to stress the sheer complexity of political life – and the unpredictability of its outcomes. He is therefore constantly on his guard against easy nostrums and instant cures for deep-seated problems. If, on the one hand, such caution can help to protect corruption and abuses (and Burke was well aware of the scandals of eighteenth-century public administration), it also saved the country from much worse disasters:

The science of constructing a commonwealth, or renovating it, or reforming it, is, like every other experimental science, not to be taught *a priori*. Nor is it a short experience that can instruct us in that practical science; because the real effects of moral causes are not always immediate; but that which in the first instance is prejudicial may be excellent in its remoter operation; and its excellence may arise even from the ill effects it produces in the beginning. The reverse also happens; and very plausible schemes, with very pleasing commencements, have often shameful and lamentable conclusions. In states there are often some obscure and almost latent causes, things which appear at first view of little moment, on which a very great part of its prosperity or adversity may most essentially depend. The science of government being therefore so practical in itself, and intended for such practical purposes, a matter which requires experience, and even more experience than any person can gain in his whole life, however sagacious and observing he may be, it is with infinite caution that any man ought to venture upon pulling down an edifice which has answered in any tolerable degree for ages the common purposes of society, or on building it up again, without having models and patterns of approved utility before his eyes.

These metaphysic rights entering into common life, like rays of light which pierce into a dense medium, are, by the laws of nature, refracted from their straight line. Indeed in the gross and complicated mass of human passions and concerns, the primitive rights of men undergo such a variety of refractions and reflections, that it becomes absurd to talk of them as if they continued in the simplicity of their original direction. The nature of man is intricate; the objects of society are of the greatest possible complexity; and therefore no simple disposition or direction of power can be suitable either to man's nature, or to the quality of his affairs. When I hear the simplicity of contrivance aimed at and boasted of in any new political constitutions, I am at no loss to decide that the artificers are grossly ignorant of their trade, or totally negligent of their duty. The simple governments are fundamentally defective, to say no worse of them. If you were to contemplate society in but one point of view, all these simple modes of polity are infinitely captivating. In effect each would answer its single end much more perfectly than the more complex is able to attain all its complex purposes. But it is better that the whole should be imperfectly and anomalously answered, than that, while some parts are provided for with great exactness, others might be totally neglected, or perhaps materially injured, by the over-care of a favourite member. . . .

To avoid therefore the evils of inconstancy and versatility, ten thousand times worse than those of obstinacy and the blindest prejudice, we have consecrated the state, that no man should approach to look into its defects or corruptions but with due caution; that he should never dream of beginning its reformation by its subversion; that he should approach to the faults of the state as to the wounds of a father, with pious awe and trembling solicitude. By this wise prejudice we are taught to look with horror on those children of their country who are prompt rashly to hack that aged parent in pieces, and put him into the kettle of magicians, in hopes that by their poisonous weeds, and wild incantations, they may regenerate the paternal constitution, and renovate their father's life.

Ibid., pp.90–91, 143.

Though Burke's argument has become the classic statement of the conservative case, it is important to stress that it was not necessarily seen as such in his own time. In spite of the fact that much of his rhetoric is aristocratic in tone, its substance is middle-class. Statesmanship is indeed the prerogative of class, but it is a class based on talent, not on birth. Burke is never entirely unaware of his own humble origins. For him the social stability essential for true civilisation is dependent upon two principles: what he designates 'the spirit of a gentleman, and the spirit of religion' (p.117). With hindsight both seem to belong more firmly to the Victorian world of bourgeois virtues than to that of Burke's own more aristocratic eighteenth century – but, of course, it is Burke who helped to make them so.

What links these essential qualities of civilisation with politics for Burke is that they stand for what he sees as eternal truths rather than the dictates of passing fashion. His basic metaphor for society is that of an organism: often more specifically conceived of as that king of the forest, an oak tree. We shelter beneath its branches; the streams that feed it must be kept pure and unpolluted; its acorns, the 'fruits' of learning, must not 'be cast into the mire, and trodden down under the hoofs of a swinish multitude'; and even commerce, trade and manufacture 'grew under the same shade in which learning flourished' (pp.117–18). An organism such as a tree is long-living, greater than the life-span of the individuals who benefit from it, but it is susceptible to violent shocks and changes. Though change is certainly possible, and indeed change is inseparable from the twin processes of growth and decay inherent in any organism, that change is always gradual and slow, a product of what would nowadays be called evolution rather than revolution:

> Society is indeed a contract. Subordinate contracts for objects of mere occasional interest may be dissolved at pleasure – but the state ought not to be considered as nothing better than a partnership agreement in a trade of pepper and coffee, callico or tobacco, or some other such low concern, to be taken up for a little temporary interest, and to be dissolved by the fancy of the parties. It is to be looked on with other reverence; because it is not a partnership in things subservient only to the gross animal existence of a temporary and perishable nature. It is a partnership in all science; a partnership in all art; a partnership in every virtue, and in all perfection. As the ends of such a partnership cannot be obtained in many generations, it becomes a partnership not only between those who are living, but between those who are living, those who are dead, and those who are to be born. Each contract of each particular state is but a clause in the great primaeval contract of eternal society, linking the lower with the higher natures, connecting the visible and invisible world, according to a fixed compact sanctioned by the inviolable oath which holds all physical and all moral natures, each in their appointed

place. This law is not subject to the will of those, who by an obligation above them, and infinitely superior, are bound to submit their will to that law. The municipal corporations of that universal kingdom are not morally at liberty at their pleasure, and on their speculations of a contingent improvement, wholly to separate and tear asunder the hands of their subordinate community, and to dissolve it into an unsocial, uncivil, unconnected chaos of elementary principles. It is the first and supreme necessity only, a necessity that is not chosen but chooses, a necessity paramount to deliberation, that admits no discussion, and demands no evidence, which alone can justify a resort to anarchy. This necessity is no exception to the rule; because this necessity itself is a part too of that moral and physical disposition of things to which man must be obedient by consent or force; but if that which is only submission to necessity should be made the object of choice, the law is broken, nature is disobeyed, and the rebellious are outlawed, cast forth, and exiled, from this world of reason, and order, and peace, and virtue, and fruitful penitence, into the antagonist world of madness, discord, vice, confusion, and unavailing sorrow.

Ibid., pp.143–45.

We must keep faith not merely with the living but also with the dead and the unborn. Once again Burke is thinking of 'liberty' as a property to be handed down from generation to generation. No man is an island . . . .

Corporate bodies are immortal for the good of the members, but not for their punishment. Nations themselves are such corporations. As well might we in England think of waging inexpiable war upon all Frenchmen for the evils which they have brought upon us in the several periods of our mutual hostilities. You might, on your part, think yourselves justified in falling upon all Englishmen on account of the unparalleled calamities brought upon the people of France by the unjust invasions of our Henries and our Edwards. Indeed we should be mutually justified in this exterminatory war upon each other, full as much as you are in the unprovoked persecution of your present countrymen, on account of the conduct of men of the same name in other times.

We do not draw the moral lessons we might from history. . . . In history a great volume is unrolled for our instruction, drawing the materials of future wisdom from the past errors and infirmities of mankind. . . . History consists, for the greater part, of the miseries brought upon the world by pride, ambition, avarice, revenge, lust, sedition, hypocrisy, ungoverned zeal, and all the train of disorderly appetites, which shake the public with the same

   – troublous storms that toss
The private state, and render life unsweet.

Ibid., pp.208–9.

It is for this reason that the new constitution, the product of revolution and unsanctioned by the rule of law and the rights of inheritance, must find itself on trial in a way that the established constitution does not. Burke has no doubt that if the new French constitution were to be weighed in the balance it would be found wanting:

I have taken a review of what has been done by the governing power in France. I have certainly spoke of it with freedom. Those whose principle it is to despise the antient permanent sense of mankind, and to set up a scheme of society on new principles, must naturally expect that such of us who think better of the judgment of the human race than of theirs, should consider both them and their devices, as men and schemes upon their trial. . . .

I can never consider this assembly as any thing else than a voluntary association of men, who have availed themselves of circumstances, to seize upon the power of the state. They have not the sanction and authority of the character under which they first met. They have assumed another of a very different nature; and have completely altered and inverted all the relations in which they originally stood. They do not hold the authority they exercise under any constitutional law of the state. They have departed from the instructions of the people by whom they were sent; which instructions, as the assembly did not act in virtue of any antient usage or settled law, were the sole source of their authority. . . .

This assembly has hardly a year's prescription. We have their own word for it that they have made a revolution. To make a revolution is a measure which, *prima fronte*, requires an apology. To make a revolution is to subvert the antient state of our country; and no common reasons are called for to justify so violent a proceeding. The sense of mankind authorizes us to examine into the mode of acquiring new power, and to criticise on the use that is made of it with less awe and reverence than that which is usually conceded to a settled and recognized authority.

Ibid., pp.243–45.

There is, Burke concedes with magisterial irony, one important sense in which the revolutionary government of France has been content to abide by the ancient rule: that of tyranny. 'They proceed exactly as their ancestors of ambition have done before them. Trace them through all their artifices, frauds, and violences, you can find nothing at all that is new. They follow precedents and examples with all the punctilious exactness of a pleader. They never depart an iota from the authentic formulas of tyranny and usurpation' (p.245).

In contrast Burke presents a vision of Britain and its ancient unwritten constitution that was for many of his fellow-citizens, less well-placed than himself, almost as ironic in its assumptions of its beneficial effects and moral superiority:

Old establishments are tried by their effects. If the people are happy, united, wealthy, and powerful, we presume the rest. We conclude that to be good from whence good is derived. In old establishments various correctives have been found for their aberrations from theory. Indeed they are the results of various necessities and expediences. They are not often constructed after any theory; theories are rather drawn from them. In them we often see the end best obtained, where the means seem not perfectly reconcileable to what we may fancy was the original scheme. The means taught by experience may be better suited to political ends than those contrived in the original project. They again re-act upon the primitive constitution, and sometimes improve the design itself from which they seem to have departed. I think all this might be curiously exemplified in the British constitution. At worst, the errors and deviations of every kind in reckoning are found and computed, and the ship proceeds in her course. This is the case of old establishments; but in a new and merely theoretic system, it is expected that every contrivance shall appear, on the face of it, to answer its end; especially where the projectors are no way embarrassed with an endeavour to accommodate the new building to an old one, either in the walls or on the foundations.

Ibid., p.255.

Yet such eulogies of the condition of England were themselves signs of implicit change in a way that it is unlikely even Burke could have been conscious of. Whatever the effects of the Revolution in France, by provoking such a debate in England it had altered the situation beyond recall. No doubt Burke's use of the conditional 'if' in the second sentence was no more than a rhetorical flourish to which his readers would automatically answer 'yes'. Yet simply by inviting even such a stock response Burke has opened the way for other kinds of reply. We may accept his central thesis concerning the organic and corporate nature of the state and agree that 'old establishments are tried by their effects . . .'. But what if the proposed criteria of a happy, united, wealthy and powerful people are manifestly not met? What if the bulk of the population increasingly saw itself as oppressed and in misery? Whatever Burke might claim, it was not just the French constitution that was on trial.

William Blake

William Blake (1757–1827) is the wild card in the Revolution debate. Outside a small circle of friends and admirers his work was virtually unpublished and unknown – and of those who knew him many, even among his admirers, thought him probably mad.

Born and brought up in central London (his father was a hosier in what is now Soho), he trained as a draughtsman and at the age of fourteen apprenticed to a well-known engraver. While this education as an artist-craftsman was crucial to his later development, and gave him in many ways a better aesthetic education than a more conventional schooling might have done, it also locked him into a precarious and declining industry, already under threat by the 1790s from new technologies that were providing cheaper and faster means of graphic reproduction and which, as in so many other trades of the period, made the skills of the individual craftsman obsolete. The general decline of his trade was made worse by the fact that the man to whom he was apprenticed, James Basire, was conspicuously old-fashioned in both his style and methods. Blake was as a result professionally caught up in the social distress and economic upheavals of the Revolutionary era in a way that none of his other fellow-poets were.

The question of apprenticeship also revealed another side of his character – an apparently innate visionary and prophetic streak that was later, through his massive reading, to develop into a fully-fledged mysticism. His father had originally wanted to apprentice him to a man called Ryland, but the fourteen-year-old Blake objected on the grounds that Ryland 'looked as if he would live to be hanged', a prophecy that came true twelve years later when it was discovered that the skilled engraver was a no less skilled forger.

Blake's relative obscurity and poverty early contributed to

a vicious circle: lacking normal means of publishing and an established readership for his work, he tended increasingly not to care if his private references and personal mythology were intelligible to the public or not. Nor was the circulation of his work helped by his insistence on printing his works himself by hand from etched copper plates and colouring his designs either by colour-washes or more often by a laborious method which he had invented himself (or which, as he claimed, had been revealed to him by his dead brother in a dream).

As was mentioned in the Introduction, he was a member of the circle centring on Joseph Johnson in the 1790s that included Price, Godwin, Paine, Priestley and Wollstonecraft, and was undoubtedly better-informed than most of his contemporaries as to what was happening both in France and in the concurrent debate in England. Until September 1792, when the first massacres leading to the Reign of Terror began in France, Blake was said to be one of the very few of that pro-Revolutionary circle who dared to wear on his head in broad daylight the French *bonnet rouge* with a white cockade, the symbol of the Revolution. When news of the September Massacres reached London, he tore off his hat and never wore it again. Shortly after, according to an uncorroborated story of Blake's, he warned Paine at a meeting at Johnson's not to return home since he would be arrested, but to flee directly to France. Whether or not it was due to Blake's foreknowledge, it is certainly remarkable that Paine was able to escape arrest and leave the country. Yet given Blake's natural cast of mind and his method of working, it is not surprising that for him the Revolution should have become more an event in the history and evolution of human spiritual consciousness than simply a sequence of political events, however profoundly he was personally moved by them. Thus in even his earliest poems from the Revolutionary period (and, since he did his own engraving, it is often difficult to date his poems with exactitude) the liberation of the spirit is seen in social and apocalyptic terms – and applied directly to his own society.

The poem entitled *The French Revolution* is one of his few works to be published professionally (by Johnson, of course) and it is doubtful whether it ever went on sale – only the first of the promised seven books exists, and that only in a single set of proofs. Here, where one might expect Blake's most explicit statement on the events in France, the facts of history are totally subordinated to brooding atmospherics. It is a conflict between youth and age, sickness and health; the cycles of natural decay and regeneration are couched in apocalyptic and prophetic language – curiously unlike the sharp vision and verbal economy of the *Songs of Experience*:

> The dead brood over Europe, the cloud and vision
>   descends over chearful France;
> O cloud well appointed! Sick, sick, the Prince on his
>   couch, wreath'd in dim
> And appalling mist, his strong hand outstretch'd, from
>   his shoulder down the bone
> Runs aching cold into the scepter, too heavy for mortal
>   grasp. No more
> To be swayed by visible hand, nor in cruelty bruise
>   the mild flourishing mountains.
>
> Sick the mountains, and all their vineyards weep, in
>   the eyes of the kingly mourner;
> Pale is the morning cloud in his visage. Rise, Necker!
>   the ancient dawn calls us
> To awake from slumbers of five thousand years. I
>   awake, but my soul is in dreams;
> From my window I see the old mountains of France,
>   like aged men, fading away.
>
> Troubled, leaning on Necker, descends the King to
>   his chamber of council; shady mountains
> In fear utter voices of thunder; the woods of France
>   embosom the sound;
> Clouds of wisdom prophetic reply, and roll over the
>   palace roof heavy.
> Forty men, each conversing with woes in the infinite
>   shadows of his soul,
> Like our ancient fathers in regions of twilight, walk,
>   gathering round the King;
> Again the loud voice of France cries to the morning;
>   the morning prophecies to its clouds.

The French Revolution, Book the First, ll.1–15.

In *America*, which was not in fact engraved until 1793, the perpetual struggle between liberty and repression that Blake seems to see as inherent in the human condition, is symbolised by the conflict between Britain and the United States – the country of Washington, Franklin, and – Paine.

> The Guardian Prince of Albion burns in his nightly
>   tent:
> Sullen fires across the Atlantic glow to America's
>   shore,
> Piercing the souls of warlike men who rise in silent
>   night.
> Washington, Franklin, Paine & Warren, Gates, Han-
>   cock & Green
> Meet on the coast glowing with blood from Albion's
>   fiery Prince.
> Washington spoke: 'Friends of America! look over the
>   Atlantic sea;
> 'A bended bow is lifted in heaven, & a heavy iron
>   chain
> 'Descends, link by link, from Albion's cliffs across the
>   sea, to bind
> 'Brothers & sons of America till our faces pale and
>   yellow,
> 'Heads deprest, voices weak, eyes downcast, hands
>   work-bruis'd,
> 'Feet bleeding on the sultry sands, and the furrows of
>   the whip
> 'Descend to generations that in future times forget.'
>
> The strong voice ceas'd, for a terrible blast swept over
>   the heaving sea:
> The eastern cloud rent: on his cliffs stood Albion's
>   wrathful Prince,
> And flam'd red meteors round the land of Albion
>   beneath;
> His voice, his locks, his awful shoulders, and his
>   glowing eyes.

ll.1–17.

'The morning comes, the night decays, the watchmen
leave their stations;
'The grave is burst, the spices shed, the linen wrapped
up;
'The bones of death, the cov'ring clay, the sinews
shrunk & dry'd
'Reviving shake, inspiring move, breathing, awaken-
ing,
'Spring like redeemed captives when their bonds &
bars are burst.
'Let the slave grinding at the mill run out into the
field,
'Let him look up into the heavens & laugh in the
bright air;
'Let the inchained soul, shut up in darkness and in
sighing,
'Whose face has never seen a smile in thirty weary
years,
'Rise and look out; his chains are loose, his dungeon
doors are open;
'And let his wife and children return from the oppressor's scourge.

'They look behind at every step & believe it is a dream,
'Singing: "The Sun has left his blackness & has found
a fresher morning,
'"And the fair Moon rejoices in the clear & cloudless
night;
'"For Empire is no more, and now the Lion & Wolf
shall cease."'

                                                    ll.1–15.

The French Revolution for Blake, so far from being a one-
off event, is only the latest manifestation of a perpetual
struggle that is not merely political but which is also waged
within the psyche itself between eternal 'contraries' without
which (as he says in another work of the same period,
The Marriage of Heaven and Hell) there would be 'no
progression'.

Tom Paine

Tom Paine (1737–1809) was perhaps Burke's most formidable antagonist. Born in Thetford (Norfolk) of Quaker stock, he worked first of all in his father's business as a sailmaker and then at the age of nineteen joined a privateer. In 1761 he became a customs officer first in Thetford and then in Lewes (Sussex). Dismissed in 1774 for agitation leading to a petition to parliament in support of a pay claim, Paine left for America with an introduction to Franklin.

In America he rapidly took up the Colonists' cause, publishing a pamphlet on the subject, *Common Sense* (1776), and later joined the revolutionary army. His American period was formative not merely in giving him actual experience of a successful revolution and the setting up of an alternative and more democratic political system, but also in linguistic terms. This was the period when the lexicographer Noah Webster, compiler of the first American dictionary, was producing the simplified system of spelling now standard in the USA and with it a trenchant critique of the literary and classicist style favoured by the English educated classes of the time and given authority by Johnson's dictionary.

The fruits of this were rapidly to become apparent after Paine's return to England in 1787 with the publication of his famous reply to Burke, *The Rights of Man*. This was published by Joseph Johnson and dedicated with deliberate bravado to George Washington. It came out in two parts, Part I in February 1791 and Part II exactly a year later, both rapidly outstripping the *Reflections* in terms of sales. The total figures are a matter of dispute, but we know that Part I, which cost three shillings, sold fifty thousand copies in 1791. When it was reprinted with the publication of Part II in February 1792, both parts were sold at sixpence each. Paine himself estimated in 1809, just before his death, that his total sales were as much as one and a half million, but most modern commentators are inclined to reduce this figure by up to a factor of ten: what is certainly true is that Part II comfortably outsold Part I. Since the second part is less concerned with the French Revolution than with what an egalitarian society in general might look like, the effect of this imbalance in sales was to shift still further the area of debate away from the rights and wrongs of the rapidly-changing situation in France and towards the situation in England. A passage from Chapter 4 of Part II, on kingship, illustrates clearly the political dangers, from the government point of view, of this tendency to generalise the argument and to take it by implication out of the French context and apply it nearer home:

> When extraordinary power and extraordinary pay are allotted to any individual in a government, he becomes the center around which every kind of corruption generates and forms. Give to any man a million a year, and add thereto the power of creating and disposing of places, at the expence of a country, and the liberties of that country are no longer secure. What is called the splendor of a throne is no other than the corruption of the state. It is made up of a band of parasites, living in luxurious indolence, out of the public taxes.

p.448.

It was hardly surprising that after the publication of the second part Paine had to flee to France to avoid prosecution. There he was welcomed as a champion of liberty and, in tune with the 'internationalist' outlook of this stage of the Revolution, in August 1792 he was made an honorary French citizen and in September elected to the National Assembly. Here, however, he fell foul of the very processes Burke had predicted. In spite of his opinion of kings ('What is called monarchy, always appears to me a silly, contemptible thing'), he opposed the execution of Louis XVI and in December 1793 he himself was arrested. His life was saved only by the fall of Robespierre. He was released in November 1794. During his time in gaol he was able to complete the second part of *The Age of Reason*, an outspoken attack on religion in general and Christianity in particular, the first part of which had appeared in 1793. In 1802 he returned to America where he died seven years later.

Paine's attack on Burke is itself a skilled piece of rhetoric. He begins by summarising the existing state of the debate:

Among the incivilities by which nations or individuals provoke and irritate each other, Mr. Burke's pamphlet on the French Revolution is an extraordinary instance. Neither the people of France, nor the National Assembly, were troubling themselves about the affairs of England, or the English Parliament; and that Mr. Burke should commence an unprovoked attack upon them, both in parliament and in public, is a conduct that cannot be pardoned on the score of manners, nor justified on that of policy.

There is scarcely an epithet of abuse to be found in the English language, with which Mr. Burke has not loaded the French nation and the National Assembly. Everything which rancour, prejudice, ignorance or knowledge could suggest, is poured forth in the copious fury of near four hundred pages. In the strain and on the plan Mr. Burke was writing, he might have written on to as many thousands. When the tongue or the pen is let loose in a phrenzy of passion, it is the man, and not the subject, that becomes exhausted.

Hitherto Mr. Burke has been mistaken and disappointed in the opinions he had formed of the affairs of France; but such is the ingenuity of his hope, or the malignancy of his despair, that it furnishes him with new pretences to go on. There was a time when it was impossible to make Mr. Burke believe there would be any Revolution in France. His opinion then was, that the French had neither spirit to undertake it nor fortitude to support it; and now that there is one, he seeks an escape by condemning it.

Rights of Man, Part I, p.275.

From this general summary he moves on to deal with what he sees as the particulars of Burke's argument, which Paine sees as a mixture of subtle misrepresentation of Price and a general mystical obfuscation of the real issues:

Not sufficiently content with abusing the National Assembly, a great part of his work is taken up with abusing Dr. Price (one of the best-hearted men that lives) and the two societies in England known by the name of the Revolution Society and the Society for Constitutional Information.

Dr. Price had preached a sermon on the 4th of November, 1789, being the anniversary of what is called in England the Revolution, which took place in 1688. Mr. Burke, speaking of this sermon, says, 'The political Divine proceeds dogmatically to assert, that by the principles of the Revolution, the people of England have acquired three fundamental rights:

1. To choose our own governors.
2. To cashier them for misconduct.
3. To frame a government for ourselves.'

Dr. Price does not say that the right to do these things exists in this or in that person, or in this or in that description of persons, but that it exists in the *whole*: that it is a right resident in the nation. Mr. Burke, on the contrary denies that such a right exists in the nation, either in whole or in part, or that it exists anywhere; and, what is still more strange and marvellous, he says, 'that the people of England utterly disclaim such a right, and that they will resist the practical assertion of it with their lives and fortunes.' That men should take up arms and spend their lives and fortunes, *not to* maintain their rights, but to maintain they have not rights, is an entirely new species of discovery, and suited to the paradoxical genius of Mr. Burke.

The method which Mr. Burke takes to prove that the people of England have no such rights, and that such rights do not now exist in the nation, either in whole or in part, or anywhere at all, is of the same marvellous and monstrous kind with what he has already said; for his arguments are that the persons, or the generation of persons, in whom they did exist, are dead, and with them the right is dead also.

Ibid., Part I, pp.275–76.

Price is, however, soon left behind as Paine warms to his theme. Interestingly, in view of the common image of him as a revolutionary, Paine's argument is, in its own way, as legalistic as Burke's. Burke knew perfectly well that in the absence of a written constitution the British Parliament is not in fact legally bound by ancient statutes, and to talk of such things as an inheritance to be handed down to future generations is for Paine both meaningless and dangerous:

> The parliament of the people of 1688, or of any other period, had no more right to dispose of the people of the present day, or to bind or controul them *in any shape whatever*, than the parliament or the people of the present day have to dispose of, bind or controul those who are to live a hundred or a thousand years hence. Every generation is, and must be, competent to all the purposes which its occasions require. It is the living, and not the dead, that are to be accommodated. When man ceases to be, his power and his wants cease with him; and having no longer any participation in the concerns of this world, he has no longer any authority in directing who shall be its governors, or how its government shall be organized, or how administered.
>
> Ibid., Part I, p.278.

Moreover, there is, Paine observes, a curious gap in Burke's discussion of revolutions: he makes no mention of America. Yet the newly independent United States, of which Paine, unlike Burke, had first-hand experience, was by no means the lawless tyranny governed by power alone that Burke's argument might lead one to suppose. He counters Burke's attempt to seize for his own purposes the potent appeal to nature by a Rousseauistic vision of the development of the natural man in the New World, freed from the artificialities and constraints of the Old:

> The independence of America, considered merely as a separation from England, would have been a matter

of but little importance, had it not been accompanied by a revolution in the principles and practice of governments. She made a stand, not for herself only, but for the world, and looked beyond the advantages herself could receive. Even the Hessian, though hired to fight against her, may live to bless his defeat; and England, condemning the viciousness of its government, rejoice in its miscarriage.

As America was the only spot in the political world where the principle of universal reformation could begin, so also was it the best in the natural world. An assemblage of circumstances conspired not only to give birth, but to add gigantic maturity to its principles. The scene which that country presents to the eye of a spectator has something in it which generates and encourages great ideas. Nature appears to him in magnitude. The mighty objects he beholds act upon his mind by enlarging it, and he partakes of the greatness he contemplates. Its first settlers were emigrants from different European nations, and of diversified professions of religion, retiring from the governmental persecutions of the old world, and meeting in the new, not as enemies, but as brothers. The wants which necessarily accompany the cultivation of a wilderness produced among them a state of society which countries long harassed by the quarrels and intrigues of governments had neglected to cherish. In such a situation man becomes what he ought. He sees his species, not with the inhuman idea of a natural enemy, but as kindred; and the example shows to the artificial world that man must go back to nature for information.

Ibid., Part II, Introduction, pp.401–2.

Burke's appeal to history, besides being spuriously legalistic, is also spurious history. The benevolent and paternalistic system envisaged by Burke as the guardian of the true liberties of society is the version of those in power. In reality it is nothing more than the assumption and retention of power by a small group for its own interests. In this it is directly opposed to the needs and the wishes of the mass of the people:

> Nothing can appear more contradictory than the principles on which the old governments began, and the condition to which society, civilization, and commerce are capable of carrying mankind. Government, on the old system, is an assumption of power, for the aggrandizement of itself; on the new a delegation of power for the common benefit of society. The former supports itself by keeping up a system of war; the latter promotes a system of peace, as the true means of enriching a nation. The one encourages national prejudices; the other promotes universal society, as the means of universal commerce. The one measures its prosperity by the quantity of revenue it extorts; the other proves its excellence by the small quantity of taxes it requires.
>
> ... Though it might be proved that the system of government now called the NEW is the most ancient in principle of all that have existed, being founded on the original inherent Rights of Man; yet, as tyranny and the sword have suspended the exercises of those rights for many centuries past, it serves better the purpose of distinction to call it the *new* than to claim the right of calling it the old.
>
> The first general distinction between those two systems is that the one now called the old is *hereditary*, either in whole or in part; and the new is entirely *representative*. It rejects all hereditary government:
>
> First, As being an imposition on mankind.
>
> Secondly, As inadequate to the purposes for which government is necessary.
>
> With respect to the first of these heads – It cannot be proved by what right hereditary government could begin; neither does there exist within the compass of mortal power a right to establish it. Man has no authority over posterity in matters of personal right; and, therefore, no man or body of men had, or can have, a right to set up hereditary government. Were

even ourselves to come again into existence, instead of being succeeded by posterity, we have not now the right of taking from ourselves the rights which would then be ours. On what ground, then, do we pretend to take them from others?

All hereditary government is in its nature tyranny. An heritable crown, or an heritable throne, or by what other fanciful name such things may be called, have no other significant explanation than that mankind are heritable property. To inherit a government, is to inherit the people, as if they were flocks and herds.

With respect to the second head, that of being inadequate to the purposes for which government is necessary, we have only to consider what government essentially is, and compare it with the circumstances to which hereditary succession is subject.

Government ought to be a thing always in full maturity. It ought to be so constructed as to be superior to all the accidents to which individual man is subject; and, therefore, hereditary succession, by being *subject to them all*, is the most irregular and imperfect of all the systems of government.

Ibid., Part II, Ch. III, pp.413–15.

Paine now turns his concentrated wit and venom upon the monarchy. Though he does not mention George III or indeed the British Crown in general, his drift is absolutely clear. The Hanoverian monarchy was at best an unglamorous affair (the first two Georges could hardly speak English) and had never been a popular institution in the way that Victoria was to make it the following century. Shelley's description of George III in 1819 as an 'old mad, blind, despised, and dying king' if cruel, was hardly unfair. Though George had never been noted for his intelligence or political astuteness and was increasingly given to fits of madness and though his son's behaviour was little short of a national disgrace, the Crown did, however, still wield real political influence, if not on the scale of the French king. The prime minister held power only with royal approval, and the one then in power, William Pitt the Younger, had gained office in 1783 at the astonishingly early age of 25 as the direct protégé of the king and against the wishes of the majority of even the unrepresentative House of Commons:

> We have heard the *Rights of Man* called a *levelling* system; but the only system to which the word *levelling* is truly applicable, is the hereditary and monarchical system. It is a system of *mental levelling*. It indiscriminately admits every species of character to the same authority. Vice and virtue, ignorance and wisdom, in short, every quality, good or bad, is put on the same level. Kings succeed each other, not as rationals, but as animals. It signifies not what their mental or moral characters are. Can we then be surprised at the abject state of the human mind in monarchical countries, when the government itself is formed on such an abject levelling system? It has no fixed character. To-day it is one thing; to-morrow it is something else. It changes with the temper of every succeeding individual, and is subject to all the varieties of each. It is government through the medium of passions and accidents. It appears under all the various characters of childhood, decrepitude, dotage; a thing at nurse, in leading-strings, or in crutches. It reverses the wholesome order of nature. It occasionally puts children over men, and the conceits of nonage over wisdom and experience. In short, we cannot conceive a more ridiculous figure of government, than hereditary succession, in all its cases, presents.
>
> . . . Passing over for the present all the evils and mischiefs which monarchy has occasioned in the world, nothing can more effectually prove its uselessness in a state of civil government, than making it hereditary. Would we make any office hereditary that required wisdom and abilities to fill it? and where wisdom and abilities are not necessary, such an office, whatever it may be, is superfluous or insignificant.
>
> Hereditary succession is a burlesque upon monarchy. It puts it in the most ridiculous light, by presenting

it as an office which any child or idiot may fill. It requires some talents to be a common mechanic; but to be a king requires only the animal figure of man – a sort of breathing automation. This superstition may last a few years more, but it cannot long resist the awakened reason and interest of men.

As to Mr. Burke, he is a stickler for monarchy, not altogether as a pensioner, if he is one, which I believe, but as a political man. He has taken up a contemptible opinion of mankind, who, in their turn, are taking up the same of him. He considers them as a herd of beings that must be governed by fraud, effigy, and show; and an idol would be as good a figure of monarchy with him as a man. I will, however, do him the justice to say that, with respect to America, he has been very complimentary. He always contended, at least in my hearing, that the people of America were more enlightened than those of England, or of any country in Europe; and that therefore the imposition of shew was not necessary in their governments.

Ibid., Part II, Ch. III, pp.415–17.

For Paine Burke's argument was a piece of intellectual dishonesty. His apparent contempt for the good sense of the ordinary people is shown by the way in which he thinks they will be taken in by a nonsense which he himself, as a man of intelligence, cannot possibly believe in. Moreover, Paine believes Burke is a 'pensioner', that is, he receives a salary or pension for writing in defence of the monarchy. In the absence of 'open government' this can only be a guess on Paine's part, but clearly the charge that he is hired to write as he does is a damning one. This would explain too Burke's turns and twists of logic when, for instance, he explains the apparent stability of American democracy in the teeth of all his dire predictions by claiming that they were 'more enlightened' than their European counterparts because they were not taken in by the farce of monarchy.

Having thus glanced at a few of the defects of the

old, or hereditary systems of government, let us compare it with the new, or representative system.

The representative system takes society and civilization for its basis; nature, reason, and experience for its guide.

Experience, in all ages and in all countries, has demonstrated that it is impossible to controul nature in her distribution of mental powers. She gives them as she pleases. Whatever is the rule by which she, apparently to us, scatters them among mankind, that rule remains a secret to man. It would be as ridiculous to attempt to fix the hereditaryship of human beauty as of wisdom. Whatever wisdom constituently is, it is like a seedless plant; it may be reared when it appears, but it cannot be voluntarily produced. There is always a sufficiency somewhere in the general mass of society for all purposes; but with respect to the parts of society, it is continually changing its place. It rises in one to-day, in another to-morrow, and has most probably visited in rotation every family of the earth, and again withdrawn.

As this is in the order of nature, the order of government must necessarily follow it, or government will, as we see it does, degenerate into ignorance. The hereditary system, therefore, is as repugnant to human wisdom as to human rights; and is as absurd as it is unjust.

As the republic of letters brings forward the best literary productions, by giving to genius a fair and universal chance; so the representative system of government is calculated to produce the wisest laws, by collecting wisdom from where it can be found. I smile to myself when I contemplate the ridiculous insignificance into which literature and all the sciences would sink, were they made hereditary; and I carry the same idea into governments. An hereditary governor is as inconsistent as an hereditary author. I know not whether Homer or Euclid had sons; but I will venture an opinion that if they had, and had left their works unfinished, those sons could not have completed them.

1. Jacques-Louis David, *The Oath of the Horatii,* 1785.

2. Jacques-Louis David, *The Oath of the Tennis Court, 20th June 1789.*

3. Jacques-Louis David, *The Death of Marat*, c. 1794.

4. Jean-Joseph-Xavier Bidauld, *View of the Town of Avezzano in the Kingdom of Naples*, 1789.

"A distant age asks where the fabric stood."

THIS IS THE HOUSE THAT JACK BUILT.

i

—— "Not to understand a treasure's worth,
Till time has stolen away the slighted good,
Is cause of half the poverty we feel,
And makes the world the wilderness it is."

THIS IS

THE WEALTH

that lay

In the House that Jack built.

ii

B

—— "A race obscene,
Spawn'd in the muddy beds of Nile, came forth,
Polluting Egypt : gardens, fields, and plains,
Were cover'd with the pest ;
The croaking nuisance lurk'd in every nook ;
Nor palaces, nor even chambers, 'scap'd ;
And the land stank—so num'rous was the fry.

THESE ARE

THE VERMIN

That Plunder the Wealth,
That lay in the House,
That Jack built.

iii

—— "Great offices will have
Great talents."

This is THE MAN—all shaven and shorn,
All cover'd with Orders—and all forlorn ;

iv

5. Illustrations to *The House that Jack Built* by William Hone, 1819.

   i Frontispiece — The Constitution is represented as a classical temple surmounted by Liberty who holds something suspiciously like a French Revolutionary bonnet on the end of her spear.

   ii The Wealth — Though this is a 'radical' pamphlet, notice how Hone's image follows Burke's metaphor in suggesting that the liberties of the English people constitute a family legacy and are, in that sense, 'property'.

   iii The Vermin — In view of the fact that the book in the 'wealth' illustration looks like a Bible, it is clearly part of Hone's ironic strategy that the central figure here is a fat clergyman — clutching just such a Bible to bolster his authority.

   iv The Dandy of Sixty — The Prince Regent's fatness and vulgarity (hence the peacock feathers) were by-words, and a gift to cartoonists. Notice, too, how the supposed sword in his left hand looks more like a crutch for his gout.

THE REAL
OR
CONSTITUTIONAL HOUSE
THAT
JACK BUILT.

" Look on this Picture, and on that."

WITH TWELVE CUTS.

THIRTEENTH EDITION.

London:
PRINTED FOR J. ASPERNE, CORNHILL;
AND
W. SAMS, St. JAMES's STREET.
1820.
Price One Shilling.

"I sought it, and its place could no where be found."

"A distant age will find the fabric good.

THIS IS THE HOUSE THAT JACK BUILT.

6.

7.

"On this foundation Faith's high temple stands,
As Atlas fix'd, not rais'd by mortal hands."

THESE ARE
THE LAWS OF ENGLAND.

8.

6. Frontispiece to *A Parody on the Political House that Jack Built* by M. Adams, 1820.

An exercise in architectural metaphor. Compare this work with Hone's original frontispiece: the implication seems to be that the *theoretical* monument is liable to be washed away in tempestuous times whereas the building in the lower illustration is, by contrast, a house for living in.

7. Frontispiece to *The Real Constitutional House that Jack Built*, Anon, 1820.

A 'throne' is composed of a map of the solar system (the 'real' meaning of *revolution*), the Bible, Law, and the Constitution.

8. Frontispiece to *The Loyalists House that Jack Built*, Anon, 1820.

A more schematised icon: The Union Jack (still recent enough to suggest the Union of England, Scotland, Ireland and Wales) is anchored (a visual metaphor also suggesting the victorious navy) to a constitutional pyramid (possibly also symbolising its age and endurance).

Do we need a stronger evidence of the absurdity of hereditary government than is seen in the descendants of those men, in any line of life, who once were famous? Is there scarcely an instance in which there is not a total reverse of the character? It appears as if the tide of mental faculties flowed as far as it could in certain channels, and then forsook its course and arose in others. How irrational then is the hereditary system, which establishes channels of power, in company with which wisdom refuses to flow! By continuing this absurdity, man is perpetually in contradiction with himself; he accepts, for a king, or a chief magistrate, or a legislator, a person whom he would not elect for a constable.

It appears to general observation that revolutions create genius and talents; but those events do no more than bring them forward. There is existing in man a mass of sense lying in a dormant state, and which, unless something excites to action, will descend to him, in that condition, to the grave. As it is to the advantage of society that the whole of its faculties should be employed, the construction of government ought to be such as to bring forward by a quiet and regular operation, all that extent of capacity which never fails to appear in revolutions.

Ibid., Part II, Ch. III, pp.418–20.

Not content with assuming the high moral ground, Burke had attempted to invoke civilisation itself, supported by nature, reason and experience in support of his defence of the *status quo*. Paine now sets out systematically to strip him of each of these props by a technique as devastating as it is witty. Burke's attempt to co-opt nature, reason and experience in support of his arguments is exposed by taking the argument directly to literature – to the very heart of the 'civilization' that he so values. Burke was, after all, as much a professional man of letters as a politician. He had been out of office for almost his entire career and could claim very little actual experience of government. On the other hand, he had been well known as the author of the *Enquiry in the Sublime and the Beautiful* and his literary reputation had been further enhanced by the enormous success of the *Reflections*. By suggesting we might as well have hereditary authorship as hereditary monarchy Paine is managing to imply that with this example he is taking the matter nearer home to Burke, who perhaps will appreciate it the better since he knows a good deal more about literature than he evidently knows about politics. There is another target concealed here too. Pitt, the prime minister, not merely owed his position to nakedly exercised royal favour, but was himself part of a political dynasty: his father had been an outstanding prime minister earlier in the century and, Paine manages to imply, the son owes his present office, not to his unaided talents but to the pernicious workings of the hereditary principle at not one, but *two* levels:

> Whether I have too little sense to see, or too much to be imposed upon; whether I have too much or too little pride, or of anything else, I leave out of the question; but certain it is, that what is called monarchy, always appears to me a silly contemptible thing. I compare it to something kept behind a curtain, about which there is a great deal of bustle and fuss, and a wonderful air of seeming solemnity; but when, by an accident, the curtain happens to be opened, and the company see what it is, they burst into laughter.
>
> In the representative system of government, nothing of this can happen. Like the nation itself, it possesses a perpetual stamina, as well of body as of mind, and presents itself on the open theatre of the world in a fair and manly manner. Whatever are its excellencies or defects, they are visible to all. It exists not by fraud and mystery; it deals not in cant and sophistry; but inspires a language that, passing from heart to heart, is felt and understood.
>
> We must shut our eyes against reason, we must basely degrade our understanding, not to see the folly of what is called monarchy. Nature is orderly in all her works; but this is a mode of government that

counteracts nature. It turns the progress of the human faculties upside down. It subjects age to be governed by children, and wisdom by folly.

On the contrary, the representative system is always parallel with the order and immutable laws of nature, and meets the reason of man in every part. For example:–

In the American federal government, more power is delegated to the President of the United States than to any other individual member of Congress. He cannot, therefore, be elected to this office under the age of thirty-five years. By this time the judgment of man becomes matured, and he has lived long enough to be acquainted with men and things, and the country with him. But on the monarchical plan (exclusive of the numerous chances there are against every man born into the world, of drawing a prize in the lottery of human faculties), the next in succession, whatever he may be, is put at the head of a nation, and of a government, at the age of eighteen years. Does this appear like an act of wisdom? Is it consistent with the proper dignity of a nation? Where is the propriety of calling such a lad the father of the people? In all other cases, a person is a minor until the age of twenty-one years. Before this period, he is not entrusted with the management of an acre of land, or with the heritable property of a flock of sheep or an herd of swine; but wonderful to tell! he may at the age of eighteen years be trusted with a nation.

That monarchy is all a bubble, a mere court artifice to procure money, is evident (at least to me) in every character in which it can be viewed. It would be impossible, on the rational system of representative government, to make out a bill of expences to such an enormous amount as this deception admits. Government is not of itself a very chargeable institution. The whole expence of the federal government of America, founded, as I have already said, on the system of representation, and extending over a country nearly ten times as large as England, is but six hundred thousand dollars, or one hundred and thirty-five thousand pounds sterling.

I presume that no man in his sober sense will compare the character of the kings of Europe with that of General Washington. Yet in France, and also in England, the expence of the civil list only, for the support of one man, is eight times greater than the whole expence of the federal government in America. To assign a reason for this appears almost impossible. The generality of the people of America, especially the poor, are more able to pay taxes than the generality of people either in France or England.

Ibid., Part II, Ch. III, pp.425–27.

Paine now turns his attention from the obvious injustice and chaos which for him is necessarily entailed in the principle of hereditary monarchy to what he sees as the logical alternative: the system of elected representatives practised in America and now in France. As before, he argues from principle rather than from concrete examples, but the force of his unstated argument is very clear. Britain does not have a representative government. The system of election to Parliament then in force was a patchwork that had grown up over the previous 150 years with no consistency beyond that of hallowed custom, which Burke had, with what for Paine was extraordinary perversity, tried to elevate into a principle itself. At one end of the spectrum there were, it is true, a few genuinely popular franchises where every householder had a vote; Westminster itself was one. At the other were what was known as 'rotten' or 'pocket' boroughs where population shifts or even geographical changes had so altered the franchise as to make the few voters that remained not merely open to bribery but habitually to expect it (hence their 'rottenness') or where the seat was simply open to nomination by the owner of the land in question (and so in his 'pocket'). Thus Old Sarum, the site of the original town of Salisbury, had not been inhabited since the Middle Ages, but still returned two members to Parliament. Even more startling were the towns of Dunwich and Ravenscar which had disappeared altogether under the sea but which were still represented in the House of Commons – courtesy of the landowner of the adjacent coastline. Such constituencies could be, and were, bought and sold by their owners, and Pitt's administration, especially in its early days, rested on the wholesale purchase of such seats by his royal patron, George III:

> But the case is, that the representative system diffuses such a body of knowledge throughout a nation, on the subject of government, as to explode ignorance and preclude imposition. The craft of courts cannot be acted on that ground. There is no place for mystery; nowhere for it to begin. Those who are not in the representation know as much of the nature of business as those who are. An affectation of mysterious importance would there be scouted. Nations can have no secrets; and the secrets of courts, like those of individuals, are always their defects.
>
> In the representative system, the reason for everything must publicly appear. Every man is a proprietor in government, and considers it a necessary part of his business to understand. It concerns his interest, because it affects his property. He examines the cost, and compares it with the advantages; and above all, he does not adopt the slavish custom of following what in other governments are called LEADERS.
>
> It can only be by blinding the understanding of man, and making him believe that government is some wonderful mysterious thing, that excessive revenues are obtained. Monarchy is well-calculated to ensure this end. It is the popery of government, a thing kept up to amuse the ignorant and quiet them into taxes.
>
> The government of a free country, properly speaking, is not in the persons, but in the laws. The enacting of those requires no great expence; and when they are administered the whole of civil government is performed – the rest is all court contrivance.
>
> Ibid., Part II, Ch. III, pp.427–28.

Charlotte Smith

Charlotte (Turner) Smith (1749–1806) was a contemporary feminist and novelist who saw something of the Revolution at first hand. Like many eighteenth-century women her formal education had ceased early – in her case at the age of twelve – and at sixteen she had been persuaded into an arranged and loveless marriage with Benjamin Smith, son of a director of the East India Company. Her second child was born when she was still seventeen. Though they were to have ten children altogether, the family was neither prosperous nor happy. In 1783 her husband was imprisoned for debt and Smith began to write for money – poetry, translations from French and, finally, novels. When Benjamin moved to France in 1784 to escape his creditors, she followed him there and published a number of translations of French works. In 1787 she left her husband to make her own living and support her family by herself, in addition to sending Benjamin occasional gifts of money. Returning to England, she became a friend of William Hayley (Blake's one-time patron), the poet Cowper and the artist Romney, and was acquainted with both Coleridge and Wordsworth (the latter of whom admired and claimed to have been influenced by her poetry).

Her novel, *Desmond* (1792), is one of the first English works of fiction to discuss the Revolution, and in her Preface she stakes a determined claim to her rights, both as a woman and a writer, to deal with political as well as domestic subjects:

> As to the political passages dispersed through the work, they are for the most part, drawn from conversations to which I have been a witness, in England, and France, during the last twelve months. In carrying on my story in those countries, and at a period when their political situation (but particularly that of the latter) is the general topic of discourse in both; I have given to my imaginary characters the arguments I have heard on both sides; and if those in favor of one party have evidently the advantage, it is not owing to my

partial representation, but to the predominant power of truth and reason, which can neither be altered nor concealed.

But women it is said have no business with politics – Why not? – Have they no interest in the scenes that are acting around them, in which they have fathers, brothers, husbands, sons, or friends engaged? – Even in the commonest course of female education, they are expected to acquire some knowledge of history; and yet, if they are to have no opinion of what *is* passing, it avails little that they should be informed of what *has passed*, in a world where they are subject to such mental degradation; where they are censured as affecting masculine knowledge if they happen to have any understanding; or despised as insignificant triflers if they have none.

Knowledge, which qualifies women to speak or to write on any other than the most common and trivial subjects, is supposed to be of so difficult attainment, that it cannot be acquired but by the sacrifice of domestic virtues, or the neglect of domestic duties. – I however may safely say, that it was in the *observance*, not in the *breach* of duty, *I* became an Author; and it has happened, that the circumstances which have compelled me to write, have introduced me to those scenes of life, and those varieties of character which I should otherwise never have seen.

> *Desmond*, (reprint, Garland Publishing, Inc. New York, 1974), Vol. 1, pp.ii–v.

Her fictional hero, Lionel Desmond, like so many of his real-life contemporaries, sees an immediate connection between the events in France and the political situation in England. The war, for instance, is both immoral and absurd. The French have on their own soil planted the 'tree of liberty', a metaphor with a long and emotive history in English radicalism supposedly reaching back to a mythical time of 'Anglo-Saxon liberties' before the Norman Conquest imposed the present class-structure on the land. It is to this tree, too, that Burke makes implicit reference in his image of the constitution as an oak tree sheltering the individual citizen:

> The enemies of the French revolution are, at present, in dismay – for the King has signed the constitution, and they begin seriously to fear that the liberties of France will be firmly established – Their great hope, however, is in the confederacy of 'the kings of the earth' against it, particularly that of the Northern powers; which, if they do unite, will be the first instance, in the annals of mankind, of an union of tyrants to crush a people who profess to have no other object than to obtain, for themselves, that liberty which is the undoubted birth-right of all mankind – I do not, my friend, fear that all 'these tyrannous breathings of the North' will destroy the lovely tree that has thus taken vigorous root in the finest country of the world, though it may awhile check its growth, and blight its produce; but I lament, that in despite of the pacific intentions of the French towards their neighbours, its root must be manured with blood – I lament still more, the disposition which too many Englishmen shew to join in this unjust and infamous *crusade* against the holy standard of freedom; and I blush for my country!
>
> Vol. III, pp.207–8.

The real area of controversy, however, centres as always around Burke and what was seen as the shameful conduct of his fellow-politicians in the government, who one minute were abusing him for his attacks on them from the opposition benches and the next were hailing his political wisdom and insight for his defence of the *status quo* in the *Reflections*. Desmond repeats the charge made by Paine that, despite his role in the opposition, Burke is really in some way in the pay of the government. Why else should he suddenly become the defender of all the abuses that he has for years been attacking?

As for his political adversaries, who have taken up the gauntlet, he has chosen to throw down – What have they done to excite such a terrible outcry? They have shewn many prejudices, which we have been so accustomed to, that we never thought of looking at them.

They have endeavoured to convince us of the absurdity and folly of war – the inefficacy of conquest – the imposition which all European nations have submitted to, who have, for ages, paid for the privilege of murdering each other – These writers have told us what, I apprehend, Locke, and Milton, and Bacon, and (what is better than all) common sense has told us before, that government is not for the benefit of the governors, but the governed; that the people are not transferrable like property; and their money is very ill bestowed, when, instead of preventing the evils of poverty, it is taken from them, to support the wanton profusion of the rich. – And what is there in all this, that in other times, Mr. Burke himself, and Mr. Burke's associates, have not repeatedly re-echoed throughout their speeches? – Once, it is certain, these gentlemen seemed to agree with Voltaire, who somewhere says,

'A mesure que les pays sont barbares, ou que les cours sont faibles, le cérémonial est plus en vogue – La vrai puissance, & la vrai politesse, dédaignent la vanité.' [In proportion as countries are rude, or their governments feeble, ceremony is more requisite – True power and true politeness alike disdain pageantry and vanity.]

Vol. III, pp.209–11.

From here it is a short step to a discussion of the monarchy itself. Whereas Paine had confined his attack to principle, Charlotte Smith is prepared to be much more specific and, in particular, to refer to the notorious life-styles of the Hanoverian Court, especially the sons of George III, who were using taxpayers' money from the Civil List to pay sinecures to a whole army of dubious hangers-on:

But let us allow, in contradiction to Mr. Burke's former opinion, (who once wished to see even the sun of royalty shorn of his superfluous beams) let us allow, that a very great degree of splendor should surround the chief magistrate of a great and opulent nation – Let us allow, that the illustrious personage, who now fills that character, has, from his private and public virtues, a claim to the warmest affections of his people; that towards him and his family, the greatest zeal and attachment should be felt, and every support of his dignity chearfully given; yet, can it be denied, that the people are enduring needless burthens, with which all this has nothing to do?

Let any man (whose name neither is, nor is ever likely to be in the court-calendar (the red book), look deliberately over it – let him reckon up the places that are there enumerated – a great many of which are sinecures – let him enquire the real amount of the salaries annexed to them, (for *they* are *not* enumerated) and the real services performed – then let him consider whether these places would exist, but for the purposes of corruption – let him reckon of how many oppressive taxes the annihilation of these places, would preclude the necessity.

I might add, that the list of pensioners, could it ever be fairly got at, might come under the same consideration – Is there upon that list *many*, are there *any* names, that have found a place there because their owners have grown old, without growing rich in the service of their country? – Does deserted merit? does indigent genius find, in the bounty of that country, an honorable resource against unmerited misfortune? Alas! no! – To those who have only *such* recommendations, the pursuit of *court favor* is hopeless indeed – But the meretricious nymph receives, with complacent smiles, the superannuated pander of a noble patron, his cast mistresses, his illegitimate children, his discarded servants, his aunts, great aunts, and fifth cousins – If the nobleman himself is a sure ministerial man in the upper house, he is sure of some degree of favor; but it is measured to him in proportion to the influence he has in the lower; and it is to reward *such men*, to gratify their dependents, that the poor pittance of the mechanic is lessened – the prices of the most necessary articles of life raised upon the 'smutched artificer,' and a share of his fourteen pence a day 'wrung from the hard hands' of the laborer.

Either these things are true, or they are not – If they are *not* true, the persons who are interested in the refutation of them, are marvellously silent! – If they *are true*, can your most enthusiastic admiration of our present glorious establishment, conceal from you, that they should be put an end to?

Vol. III, pp.207–14.

Fanny Burney

Frances Burney, Madame d'Arblay (1752–1840) was an almost exact contemporary of Charlotte Smith, but, partly through her social circle, and later, her personal circumstances, took a quite different view of the Revolution. Her father, Dr Burney, was a well-known musical historian and she was brought up in a literary and artistic circle in London that included both Dr Johnson and Burke. Her first novel, *Evelina*, had been published anonymously in 1778, but when she was revealed as its author, she became famous and eventually received a royal appointment as second Keeper of the Robes to Queen Charlotte. After resigning that post because of ill health, in 1793 she married a French émigré, General d'Arblay. From 1802 to 1812 she was interned by Napoleon in France.

From a modern reader's point of view her extensive letters, journals and diaries are as interesting as her novels for the portrait they paint of contemporary society and events. In November 1790 she wrote to a friend:

I own myself entirely of Mrs. Montagu's opinion

about Mr. Burke's book; it is the noblest, deepest, most animated, and exalted work that I think I have ever read. I am charmed to hear its *éloge* from Mrs. Montagu; it is a tribute to its excellence which reflects high honour on her own candour, as she was one of those the most vehemently irritated against its author but a short time since. How can man, with all his inequalities, be so little resembling to himself at different periods as this man? He is all ways a prodigy, – in fascinating talents and incomprehensible inconsistencies.

When I read, however, such a book as this, I am apt to imagine the whole of such a being must be right, as well as the parts, and that the time may come when the mists which obscure the motives or incentives to those actions and proceedings which may seem incongruous may be chased away, and we may find the internal intention had never been faulty, however ill appearances had supported any claim to right. Have you yet read it? You will find it to require so deep and so entire an attention, that perhaps you may delay it till in more established health; but read it you will, and with an admiration you cannot often feel excited.

Letters to Mrs Waddington, *Diary & Letters of Madame d'Arblay* (1778–1840), Vol. IV (Macmillan, 1905), pp.435–36.

In June 1792 she records in a letter a meeting and conversation with Burke:

At length – Mr. Burke appeared – accompanied by Mr. Elliot.

He shook hands with my Father, as soon as he had paid his devoirs to Mrs. Crewe, – but he returned my courtsie with so distant a Bow, that I concluded myself quite lost with him. . . . I could not wish that less obvious, thinking as I think of it; but I felt infinitely grieved to lose the favour of a Man whom, in all other articles, I so much venerate: & who, indeed, I esteem

& admire as the very first Man of true Genius now living in this Country. . . .

The moment, I was named – to my great joy I found Mr. Burke had not recollected me. He is more near-sighted, considerably, than myself. 'Miss Burney!' he now exclaimed, coming forward, &, quite kindly, taking my hand – 'I did not see you –' & then he spoke very sweet words of the meeting, & of my looking far better than *while I was a Courtier*, & of how he *rejoiced* to see that I so little suited that station. – 'You look,' cried he, 'quite *renewed* – *revived* – *disengaged* – you seemed – when I conversed with you last, at the Trial, quite – *altered* – I never saw such a change for the better as *quitting a Court* has brought about!' . . .

After this, my Father joined us, & *politics* took the lead. He [Burke] spoke then with an eagerness & vehemence that instantly banished the *Graces*, though it redoubled the *energies* of his discourse. The French Revolution, he said, which began by authorising & legalising Injustice, & which by rapid steps had pro-ceeded to every species of Despotism except owning a Despot, was now menacing all the Universe, & all Mankind with the most violent concussion of principle & order. . . .

One speech I must repeat, for it is explanatory of his conduct, & *nobly* explanatory. When he had expatiated upon the present dangers even to *English* Liberty & Property, from the contagion of Havock & novelty, he earnestly exclaimed 'THIS it is that has made *ME* an abettor & supporter of Kings! Kings are *necessary*, & if we would preserve peace & prosperity, we must preserve *THEM*. We must all put our shoulders to the Work! Aye, & stoutly, too!'

Letter to Mrs Phillips, *The Journals and Letters of Fanny Burney*, Vol. 1 (1791–1792), (Oxford, 1972), pp.194–96.

In October of the same year she wrote to her father from a

country parsonage where her host was also engaged in the current debate:

> Mr. Hawkins's house is pleasantly situated, and all that belongs to its mistress is nearly perfect. Even its master is more to my *gusto* than I have ever known him before, for he is engaged in writing notes for answers to Paine, Mackintosh, Rouse, Priestley, Price, and a score more of Mr. Burke's incendiary antagonists. I wish to spirit him on to collect them into a pamphlet and give them to the public, but he is doubtful if it would not involve him in some heavy expense. I rather think the contrary, for he has really written well, and with an animation that his style of conversation had not made me expect. It is impossible to be under the roof of an English clergyman and to witness his powers of making leisure useful, elegant, and happy, without continual internal reference to the miserable contrast of the unhappy clergy of France.
>
> Today's papers teem with the promise of great and decisive victories to the arms of the Duke of Brunswick. I tremble for the dastardly revenge menaced to the most injured King of France and his family. I dare hardly wish the advance and success of the combined armies, in the terror of such consequences. Yet the fate and future tranquillity of all Europe seem inevitably involved in the prosperity or the failure of this expedition. The depression or encouragement it must give to the political adventurers, who, at all times, can stimulate the rabble to what they please, will surely spread far, deep, and wide, according to the event of French experiment upon the minds, manners, and powers of men; and the feasibility of expunging all past experience, for the purpose of treating the world as if it were created yesterday, and every man, woman and child were let loose to act from their immediate suggestion, without reference to what is past, or sympathy in anything that is present, or precaution for whatever is to come. It seems, in truth, no longer the cause of

nations alone, but of individuals; not a dispute for a form of government, but for a condition of safety.

Letter to Dr Burney, 2 Oct 1792, *Diary & Letters of Madame d'Arblay* (1778–1840), Vol. V (Macmillan, 1905), pp.118–19.

Daniel Eaton

Among those prosecuted for selling *The Rights of Man* was Daniel Isaac Eaton (died 1814). Between 1792 and 1795 he was arrested no less than six times, though the government was unable to get juries to convict him. In November 1795 a new act was passed which enlarged the old definition of treason from specific actions to include inciting the people to hatred or contempt of the king, and printing, writing or malicious speaking with intent to harm the king. Eaton thereupon fled to America and was outlawed in his absence in 1796. On his return in 1803 he was promptly jailed for fifteen months for his earlier offences. He was prosecuted again in 1812 and 1813, but was never sentenced on account of his advanced age (it is not known exactly how old he was when he died in 1814).

As this record suggests, Eaton was one of the boldest and most outspoken critics of the British government and monarchy throughout the Revolutionary period. The title of his journal was a direct reference to Burke's notorious remark about the 'swinish multitude': *Politics for the People: a Hog's Wash or Salmagundy for Swine*. Launched in 1793, it sold for twopence and was therefore in direct competition for the popular market with tracts like those of John Reeves' loyalist Association. The ironic tone of the periodical and its outspoken political message is given by the first issue. It opens with a verse motto:

> Since Times are bad, and solid food is rare,
> The Swinish Herd should learn to live on air;
> Acorns and Pease, alas! no more abound,
> A feast of Words, is in the Hog Trough found.

Other articles in the same vein include 'The Remonstrance of the Swinish Multitude to the Chief and Deputy Swineherds of Europe'. The mixture of heavy irony and historical exposition is interspersed with extensive passages from such works as Godwin's *Political Justice*. Typical of its tone is an article entitled 'The pernicious Principles of TOM PAINE exposed, in an Address to Labourers and Mechanics. By a Gentleman'. It begins:

> You who are of the lowest class of beings that can be called MEN; to you I address myself; to you, who are the scum of the earth, and unworthy the notice of gentlemen. It is reported, and generally believed, that many of you have had the *audacity* to read books of your own chusing, without being capable of judging which were fit, and which unfit, for your perusal. . . .

Altogether *Politics for the People* dispels the notion that the French Revolution debate was separate from and earlier than the radical agitation at home. In the first number are extracts from Lord Lyttleton's 'Persian Letters', a satire on the state of Parliament and the Law in England, and an Address from the National Convention of France to the British Soldiers and Sailors:

> ENGLISHMEN, Men who have fought against and have overthrown the despotism of Monarchy, who have driven from their Country the invading Armies of two of the most powerful military nations of Europe, are still forced to fight in defence of their Liberties. Pause a while, before you resolve to make your blood flow with that of your fellow men, and consider the nature of those injuries you are come to avenge. Have the French invaded your Country? Have they interrupted your Commerce, insulted your Nation, refused to discharge towards your fellow citizens the duties of hospitality? Have you, through the wide extent of your Empire, one charge to make against the agents of the Republic? NO.

> *Politics for the People*, No. I, p.5.

For Eaton the French and British situations are closely parallel, but to France belongs the credit of having acted against the insidious corruption of hereditary rank and privilege:

> If we examine the origin of Nobility and Royal Grandeur; if we trace the genealogies of Princes and Potentates up to their first fountain, we shall find the first fathers of these noisy pedigrees to be cruel Butchers of Men, Oppressors, Tyrants, perfidious truce-breakers, Robbers, and Parricides, in a word the most primitive Nobility was no other than potent wickedness or dignified impiety.
>
> Ibid., No. III, p.26.

Accompanying such generalisations is a serial history of England from Roman times to the present, with a wealth of detailed illustration:

> Of the Royal Robbers who governed the island during these dark periods, we have a very confused account of some receiving the reward of their crimes by the hands of their own subjects; others by the hands of their fellow kings; some becoming Monks; others dying in banishment; and of one, who, though born lame, deaf, and blind, obtained the crown, by *indefeasible hereditary right*; and who first taught the people the respect that was due to Royalty, by ordering the appearance of the King to be announced by the sound of trumpets.
>
> Ibid., No. II, p.15.

Another medium favoured by Eaton as a vehicle for his irony is the traditional fable:

THE LION AND THE WOLVES.
A FABLE.

BEYOND the western verge of the earth, whence the ancient Romans, as they fancifully reported, were wont to hear the sun set in the sea with a hissing and thundering sound, there lies an Island, which for many ages was inhabited by a mighty Lion, who enjoyed all the blessings of liberty and peace in his wide domain. But in process of time, a Wolf, from the Hyrcanian forest, as he was travelling south, in search of a happier climate, heard of the happy Island inhabited by the Lion, and came to a resolution to pass over and fix his residence there. With this view he entered into a treaty with other Wolves, of whom he became the chief, and they passed over, surprised the Lion, and took him prisoner; when dreading his power and his just vengeance in case he should regain his liberty, the wolves fastened him to the ground with ropes and other instruments of oppression. They also gave him sleeping potions to keep him still, and if ever he seemed likely to become refractory, they stunned him with violent blows on the head, they made additions to the fastenings, by means of which they kept him down, every year, insomuch that those shackles spread over him like a tent or marquee, and if ever he opened his eyes a little, it was almost impossible for him to get 'a glimpse through the gloom'. The Lion continued thus as one dead for several hundred years, and the Wolves riotously and wantonly fattened on the spoils of his country. After the lapse of ages, however, the Lion accidentally received a mighty stroke of PAIN; the noise of it was like thunder, the Wolves were struck into a stupor by it, and it was said the Lion revived so far, as to move one of his ears. A second stroke of PAIN succeeded, which caused the Lion to open one of his eyes, and he began to have some thoughts of getting up from his cruel confinement. The Wolves were roused from their state of stupefaction, and howled more loudly than their brethren on the stormy steeps of Orca. They encouraged each other to apply more fastenings to the Lion. Some advised sending him out to sea and drowning him. Others were for sending him to a foreign country, where he might be knocked on the head, or buried alive. A Magpie, named Edmund, was sent to a *fist market* in the country, where he learned to call the Lion all manner of names; and in addition to all his other sufferings, dust was thrown in his eyes, in order to put them quite out, if possible.

Such was the state of things when the last accounts were received from the Lion's country, or rather the country of the Wolves, as they have usurped it – but as the Wolves had devoured all the Lion's property, it was thought some of them would decamp; and it was pretty generally believed, that all their efforts would not be sufficient to keep him down many years longer.

'The Lion and the Wolves', No. XIX (1794), pp.300–302.

With this kind of material the surprise is not that Eaton was prosecuted, but that he was so regularly acquitted by obviously sympathetic juries. The degree of revolutionary sentiment in England during this period has long been a matter of dispute, but it is not difficult to see why, after the riot in 1795 when an attempt was made on the king's life, the authorities should have resorted to draconian measures – and Eaton should have been a prime target.

Hannah More

Hannah More (1745–1833) was a prominent Evangelical author and writer of some of the most successful tracts and pamphlets of the day, appealing on the conservative side to the same kind of popular mass audience as Eaton. Her *Cheap Repository Tracts* (1795–98) cost between a penny and a penny-halfpenny and had sold two million by March 1796. It is interesting to note that, in spite of her obvious effectiveness, she was attacked by a leading conservative journal, *The Anti-Jacobin*, (and by some of her neighbours in Somerset) for encouraging the masses to read in the first place. Cobbett, on the other hand, attacked her for preaching the creed of 'the religious mouse, who lived upon dropped crumbs, and never, though ever so hungry, touched cheese or bacon on the racks or shelves.'

Her best-known work on the French Revolution and the Burke–Paine controversy is *Village Politics*, which was published in 1793 for John Reeves' Association for Preserving Liberty and Property against Republicans and Levellers – and known generally as 'The Association'. It was distributed, probably free, by the East Kent and Canterbury branches of the Association, a practice which, while by no means standard, may help to account for her phenomenal circulation figures throughout the decade.

Part of her success is due to her obvious personal sincerity, but her choice of medium is also very skilful. Just as Daniel Eaton had made good use of Aesop-like fables to illustrate his points, so More also employs a device from classical rhetoric – the Socratic dialogue. This enables her to keep a colloquial and conversational tone while avoiding the stock question-and-answer form common, for instance, for conveying information in contemporary children's books, and probably adapted from the catechism. Both participants in the dialogue are supposedly working-men, and neither is foolish enough to suggest that they live in the best of all possible worlds or that the rich are entirely blameless:

VILLAGE POLITICS
ADDRESSED
TO ALL THE MECHANICS, JOURNEYMEN
AND
DAY LABOURERS,
IN GREAT BRITAIN.

By WILL CHIP,
A COUNTRY CARPENTER.

A DIALOGUE between JACK ANVIL the
Blacksmith, and TOM HOD the Mason.

Jack. WHAT's the matter, Tom? Why dost look so dismal?

Tom. Dismal indeed! Well enough I may.

Jack. What's the old mare dead? or work scarce?

Tom. No, no, work's plenty enough, if a man had but the heart to go to it.

Jack. What book art reading? Why dost look so like a hang dog?

Tom. (*looking on his book.*) Cause enough. Why I find here that I'm very unhappy, and very miserable; which I should never have known if I had not had the good luck to meet with this book. O 'tis a precious book!

Jack. A good sign tho'; that you can't find out you're unhappy without looking into a book for it. What is the matter?

Tom. Matter? Why I want liberty.

Jack. Liberty! What has anyone fetched a warrant for thee? Come man, cheer up, I'll be bound for thee. – Thou art an honest fellow in the main, tho' thou dost tipple and prate a little too much at the Rose and Crown.

Tom. No, no, I want a new constitution.

Jack. Indeed! Why I thought thou hadst been a desperate healthy fellow. Send for the doctor then.

Tom. I'm not sick: I want Liberty and Equality, and the Rights of Man.

Jack. O now I understand thee. What thou art a leveller and a republican I warrant.

Tom. I'm a friend to the people. I want a reform.

Jack. Then the shortest way is to mend thyself.

Tom. But I want a general reform.

Jack. Then let every one mend one.

Tom. Pooh! I want freedom and happiness, the same as they have got in France.

Jack. What, Tom, we imitate them? We follow the French! Why they only begun all this mischief at first, in order to be just what we are already. Why I'd sooner go to the Negers to get learning, or to the Turks to get religion, than to the French for freedom and happiness.

Tom. What do you mean by that? ar'n't the French free?

Jack. Free, Tom! aye, free with a witness. They are all so free, that there's nobody safe. They make free to rob whom they will, and kill whom they will. If they don't like a man's looks, they make free to hang him with-out judge or jury, and the next lamp-post does for the gallows; so then they call themselves free, because you see they have no king to take them up and hang them for it.

Tom. Ah, but Jack, didn't their KING formerly hang people for nothing too? and besides, wer'n't they all papists before the Revolution?

Jack. Why, true enough, they had but a poor sort of religion, but bad is better than none, Tom. And so was the government bad enough too, for they could clap an innocent man into prison, and keep him there too as long as they would, and never say with your leave or by your leave, Gentlemen of the Jury. But what's all that to us?

Tom. To us! Why don't our governors put many of our poor folks in prison against their will? What are all the jails for? Down with the jails, I say; all men should be free.

Jack. Harkee, Tom, a few rogues in prison keep the rest in order, and then honest men go about their business, afraid of nobody; that's the way to be free. And let me tell thee, Tom, thou and I are tried by our peers as much as a lord is. Why the king can't send me to prison if I do no harm, and if I do, there's reason good why I should go there. I may go to law with Sir John, at the great castle yonder, and he no more dares lift his little finger against me than if I were his equal. A lord is hanged for hanging matter, as thou or I shou'd be; and if it will be any comfort to thee, I myself remember a Peer of the Realm being hanged for killing his man, just the same as the man wou'd have been for killing him.*

Tom. Well, that is some comfort. – But have you read the Rights of Man?

* Lord Ferrers was hanged in 1790, for killing his steward.

Jack. No, not I. I had rather by half read the *Whole Duty of Man*. I have but little time for reading, and such as I should therefore only read a bit of the best.

Tom. Don't tell me of those old fashioned notions. Why should not we have the same fine things they have got in France? I'm for a *Constitution*, and *Organization*, and *Equalization* . . .

I don't see why we are to work like slaves, while others roll about in their coaches, feed on the fat of the land, and do nothing.

Jack. My little maid brought home a story-book from the Charity-School t'other day, in which was a bit of a fable about the Belly and the Limbs. The hands said, I won't work any longer to feed this lazy belly, who sits in state like a lord, and does nothing. Said the feet, I won't walk and tire myself to carry him about; let him shift for himself, so said all the members; just as your levellers and republicans do now. And what was the consequence? Why the belly was pinched to be sure; but the hands and the feet, and the rest of the members suffered so much for want of their old nourishment, that they fell sick, pined away, and wou'd have died, if they had not come to their senses just in time to save their lives, as I hope all you will do.

Tom. But the times – but the taxes, Jack.

Jack. Things are dear, to be sure: but riot and murder is not the way to make them cheap. And taxes are high; but I'm told there's a deal of old scores paying off, and by them who did not contract the debt neither, Tom. Besides things are mending, I hope, and what little is done, is for us poor people; our candles are somewhat cheaper, and I dare say, if the honest gentleman is not disturbed by you levellers, things will mend every day. But bear one thing in mind: the more we riot, the more we shall have to pay. Mind another thing too, that in France the poor paid all the taxes, as I have heard 'em say, and the quality paid nothing.

Tom. Well, I know what's what, as well as another; and I'm as fit to govern –

Jack. No, Tom, no. You are indeed as good as another man, seeing you have hands to work, and a soul to be saved. But are all men fit for all kinds of things? Solomon says, 'How can he be wise whose talk is of oxen?' Every one in his way. I am a better judge of a horse-shoe than Sir John; but he has a deal better notion of state affairs than I; and I can no more do without him than he can do without me. And few are so poor but they may get a vote for a parliament-man, and so you see the poor have as much share in the government as they well know how to manage.

Tom. But I say all men are equal. Why should one be above another?

Jack. If that's thy talk, Tom, thou dost quarrel with Providence and not with government. For the woman is below her husband, and the children are below their mother, and the servant is below his master.

Tom. But the subject is not below the king; all kings are 'crowned ruffians:' and all governments are wicked. For my part, I'm resolved I'll pay no more taxes to any of them.

Jack. Tom, Tom, this is thy nonsense; if thou didst go oftner to church, thou wou'dst know where it is said, 'Render unto Cesar the things that are Cesar's;' and also, 'Fear God, honour the king.' Your book tells you that we need obey no government but that of the people, and that we may fashion and alter the government according to our whimsies; but mine tells me, 'Let every one be subject to the higher powers, for all power is of God, the powers that be are ordained of God; whosoever therefore resisteth the power, resisteth the ordinance of God.' Thou sayst, thou wilt pay no taxes to any of them. Dost thou know who it was that work'd a miracle, that he might have money to pay tribute with, rather than set you and me an example of disobedience to government?

Tom. I say we shall never be happy, till we do as the French have done.

Jack. The French and we contending for liberty, Tom, is just as if thou and I were to pretend to run a race; thou to set out from the starting post, when I am in already: why we've got it man; we've no race to run. We're there already. Our constitution is no more like what the French one was, than a mug of our Taunton beer is like a platter of their soup-maigre.

Tom. I know we shall be undone, if we don't get a new constitution – that's all. . . .

I don't see why one man is to ride in his coach and six, while another mends the highway for him.

Jack. I don't see why the man in the coach is to *drive over* the man on foot, or hurt a hair of his head. And as to our great folks, that you levellers have such a spite against; I don't pretend to say they are a bit better than they should be; but that's no affair of mine; let them look to that; they'll answer for that in another place. To be sure, I wish they'd set us a better example about going to church, and those things; but still *hoarding's* not the sin of the age; they don't lock up their *money* – away it goes, and every body's the better for it. They do spend too much, to be sure, in feastings and fandangoes, and if I was a parson I'd go to work with 'em in another kind of a way; but as I am only a poor tradesman, why 'tis but bringing more grist to my mill. It all comes among the people – Their coaches and their furniture, and their buildings, and their planting, employ a power of tradespeople and labourers. – Now in this village; what shou'd we do without the castle? Tho's my Lady is too rantipolish, and flies about all summer to hot water and cold water, and fresh water and salt water, when she ought to stay at home with Sir John; yet when she does come down, she brings such a deal of gentry that I have more horses than I can shoe, and my wife more linen than she can wash. Then all our grown children are servants in the family, and rare wages they have got. Our little boys get something every day by weeding their gardens, and the girls learn to sew and knit at Sir John's expence; who sends them all to school of a Sunday.

Tom. Aye, but there's not Sir Johns in every village.

Jack. The more's the pity. But there's other help.

'Twas but last year you broke your leg, and was nine weeks in the Bristol 'Firmary, where you was taken as much care of as a lord, and your family was maintained all the while by the parish. No poor-rates in France, Tom; and here there's a matter of two million and a half paid for them, if 'twas but a little better managed.

Tom. Two million and a half!

Jack. Aye, indeed. Not translated into ten-pences, as your French millions are, but twenty good shillings to the pound. But, when this levelling comes about, there will be no 'firmaries, no hospitals, no charity-schools, no sunday-schools, where so many hundred thousand poor souls learn to read the word of God for nothing. For who is to pay for them? *equality* can't afford it; and those that may be willing won't be able.

Tom. But we shall be one as good as another, for all that.

Jack. Aye, and bad will be the best. But we must work as we do now, and with this difference, that no one will be able to pay us. Tom! I have got the use of my limbs, of my liberty, of the laws, and of my Bible. The two first, I take to be my *natural* rights; the two last my *civil* and *religious*; these, I take it, are the true Rights of Man, and all the rest is nothing but nonsense and madness and wickedness. My cottage is my castle; I sit down in it at night in peace and thankfulness, and 'no man maketh me afraid.' Instead of indulging discontent, because another is richer than I in this world, (for envy is at the bottom of your equality works,) I read my bible, go to church, and think of a treasure in heaven.

Tom. Aye; but the French have got it in *this* world.

Jack. 'Tis all a lye, Tom. Sir John's butler says his master gets letters which *say* 'tis all a lye. 'Tis all murder, and nakedness, and hunger; many of the poor soldiers fight without victuals, and march without clothes. These are your *democrats!* Tom. . . .

Tom. What then dost thou take French *liberty* to be?

Jack. To murder more men in one night, than ever their poor king did in his whole life.

Tom. And what dost thou take a *Democrat* to be?

Jack. One who likes to be governed by a thousand tyrants, and yet can't bear a king.

Tom. What is *Equality*?

Jack. For every man to pull down every one that is above him, till they're all as low as the lowest.

Tom. What is *the new Rights of Man*?

Jack. Battle, murder, and sudden death.

Tom. What is to be an *enlightened people*?

Jack. To put out the light of the gospel, confound right and wrong, and grope about in pitch darkness.

Tom. What is *Philosophy*, that Tim Standish talks so much about?

Jack. To believe that there's neither God, nor devil, nor heaven, nor hell. – To dig up a wicked old fellow [Voltaire]'s rotten bones, whose books, Sir John says, have been the ruin of thousands; and to set his figure up in a church and worship him.

Tom. And what mean the other hard words that Tim talks about – *organization* and *function*, and *civism*, and *incivism*, and *equalization*, and *inviolability*, and *imperscriptible*?

Jack. Nonsense, gibberish, downright hocus-pocus. I know 'tis not English; Sir John says 'tis not Latin; and his valet de sham says 'tis not French neither.

Tom. And yet Tim says he shall never be happy till all these fine things are brought over to England.

Jack. What into this Christian country, Tom? Why dost know they have no *sabbath*? Their mob parliament meets of a Sunday to do their wicked work, as naturally as we do to go to church. They have renounced God's word and God's day, and they don't even date in the year of our Lord. Why dost turn pale, man? And the rogues are always making such a noise, Tom, in the midst of their parliament-house, that their speaker rings a bell, like our penny-postman, because he can't keep them in order.

Tom. And dost thou think our Rights of Man will lead to all this wickedness?

Jack. As sure as eggs are eggs.

Tom. I begin to think we're better off as we are.

Jack. I'm sure on't. This is only a scheme to make us go back in every thing. 'Tis making ourselves poor when we are getting rich.

Tom. I begin to think I'm not so very unhappy as I had got to fancy.

Jack. Tom, I don't care for drink myself, but thou dost, and I'll argue with thee in thy own way; when there's all equality there will be no superfluity; when there's no wages there'll be no drink; and levelling will rob thee of thy ale more than the malt-tax does.

Tom. But Standish says if we had a good government there'd be no want of any thing.

Jack. He is like many others, who take the king's money and betray him. Tho' I'm no scholar, I know that a good government is a good thing. But don't go to make me believe that any government can make a bad man good, or a discontented man happy.

Pp.1–7, 9–13, 14–18, 19–22.

3 France and England 1795–1820

PART A: ENTHUSIASM RECONSIDERED

Wordsworth and Coleridge

The word 'enthusiasm', like 'nature' and 'revolution', was in the process of changing its connotations at the end of the eighteenth century. Literally meaning (from the Greek) 'possession by a god', it had always, from its first recorded use in English in 1603, been something of an ambiguous term. Possession by a Greek god could involve divine inspiration, but it could also bring on frenzy and madness in which the possessed could commit terrible crimes, afterwards to be bitterly regretted. Throughout the eighteenth century it was more often an insult than a compliment, commonly implying a regrettable lack of self-control and sound judgement, though there were a few who were prepared to glory in the accusation – the early Methodists, for instance, or the poet Joseph Warton, who in 1744 published a poem he called *The Enthusiast: or the Lover of Nature*, which is sometimes regarded as being one of the first Romantic works. Certainly by the last quarter of the century enthusiasm had become much more respectable. Associated with other such vogue-words as 'sensibility' and 'feeling', it had become a quality commonly expected in artistic, progressive and reformist circles.

When Wordsworth, in Book IX of the 1805 *Prelude*, introduces his friend, Michel Beaupuy, the French army officer who first fired him with pro-Revolutionary zeal, he describes him, significantly, as a compendium of all those qualities:

> . . . A meeker man
> Than this lived never, or a more benign –
> Meek, though enthusiastic . . .
>   By birth he ranked
> With the most noble, but unto the poor
> Among mankind he was in service bound
> As by some tie invisible, oaths professed
> To a religious order. Man he loved
> As man, and to the mean and the obscure
> And all the homely in their homely works
> Transferred a courtesy which had no air
> Of condescension, but did rather seem
> A passion and a gallantry . . .
>   and a kind of radiant joy
> That cover'd him about when he was bent
> On works of love or freedom.

Prelude, Bk IX, ll.298–300, 309–18, 322–24.

There is, of course, a deliberate Wordsworthian irony in the application of this rhetoric of chivalry and of secular sainthood, which had been invoked so powerfully by Burke in relation to Marie Antoinette, now not merely to the 'man of feeling' but to the avowed revolutionary – and not least in binding all these traditional 'conservative' qualities together by the previously-suspect adjective 'enthusiastic'.

Wordsworth had already in earlier writings made effective use of the potential ironies inherent in the word in his (unpublished) *Letter to the Bishop of Llandaff*, written in 1793. Richard Watson (1737–1816) the Bishop of Llandaff (the diocese in which Cardiff is situated) was an interesting and controversial figure of the period. An able scientist, he had become Professor of Chemistry at Cambridge at the early age of 27 and a Fellow of the Royal Society only 5 years later. He had played an important part in the invention of the black-bulb thermometer and made improvements in the manufacture of gunpowder which were said to have saved the British government more than a hundred thousand pounds a year and contributed towards the later British victories in the Napoleonic Wars. With a flexibility only possible to an

eighteenth-century polymath he then resigned his Chair of
Chemistry in 1771 to become Regius Professor of Divinity
instead. In 1782 he left Cambridge to become Bishop of
Llandaff. Even rarer than his other accomplishments (for a
bishop) was the fact that he was a Whig with strong liberal
sympathies. He alone among the senior Anglican clergy
showed some measure of support for the early days of the
French Revolution. Even as late as January 1795 he made a
speech in the House of Lords opposing the war with France,
and predicting that

> . . . this abandonment of all religion in France will be
> followed in due time . . . by the establishment of a
> purer system of Christianity than has ever taken place
> in that country, or perhaps any country, since the age
> of the Apostles. Voltaire, Rousseau, Diderot, and the
> rest of the philosophers in France, and perhaps I may
> say, many in our own country, have mistaken the
> corruptions of Christianity for Christianity itself, and
> in spurning the yoke of superstition, have overthrown
> religion. They are in the condition of men described
> by Plutarch; they have fled from superstition; have
> leapt over religion, and sunk into Atheism. They will
> be followed by future Newtons and by future Lockes,
> who will rebuild . . . the altars which the others have
> polluted and thrown down; for they will found them
> on the pure and unadorned rock of Christian
> verity. . . .
>
> *Parl. Hist*, Vol. XXXI, p.267.

Perhaps because of these liberal sentiments, and the hopes
they aroused of support among the more radical writers and
poets, when it became clear that on the home front Watson
was solidly opposed to change, he was the subject of more
verbal abuse than any of his more conservative fellow-bishops.

It was this gap between revolutionary sympathies abroad
and complacency at home that was the subject of Wordsworth's first essay in political journalism. Turning to the
notorious sloth and inefficiency of the British legal system of

the day, he writes in the *Letter to the Bishop of Llandaff*, 'I congratulate your Lordship upon your enthusiastic fondness for the judicial proceedings of this country . . .'. A few pages before he had used the word of himself with a no-less ironic, self-deprecating modesty:

> Your Lordship tells us that the science of civil government has received all the perfection of which it is capable. For my part, I am more enthusiastic. The sorrow I feel from the contemplation of this melancholy picture is not unconsoled by a comfortable hope that the class of wretches called mendicants will not much longer shock the feelings of humanity; that the miseries entailed upon the marriage of those who are not rich will no longer tempt the bulk of mankind to fly to that promiscuous intercourse to which they are impelled by the instincts of nature, and the dreadful satisfaction of escaping the prospects of infants, sad fruit of such intercourse, whom they are unable to support. If these flattering prospects be ever realised, it must be owing to some wise and salutary regulations counteracting that inequality among mankind which proceeds from the present *forced* disproportion of their possessions.
>
> I am not an advocate for the agrarian law nor for sumptuary regulations, but I contend that the people amongst whom the law of primogeniture exists, and among whom corporate bodies are encouraged, and immense salaries annexed to useless and indeed hereditary offices, is oppressed by an inequality in the distribution of wealth which does not necessarily attend men in a state of civil society.
>
> *Prose Works*, eds W.J.B. Owen and J.W. Smyser, Vol. 1 (Oxford, 1974), pp.43–44.

One effect of the repeated use of the word 'enthusiasm' in such contexts is subtly to shift the reader's attention away from the situation under discussion and towards the state of mind of the participants – and there is no doubt that this accurately reflects a shift in the perspective of the British observers. In Wordsworth it reveals an increasing interest in the workings of his own mind as he tries to come to terms with his experiences during and immediately after the Revolution – and, by ironic extension, the mind of the poor bishop as well. In Coleridge it involves, in addition, an interest in what one might call the 'psychology of revolution' in general, and, in particular, the psychological state of the person who, more than any other, seemed to most English to embody and personify the most terrible excesses of the Revolution in France: Maximilien de Robespierre, about whom he and Southey had written a tragedy, *The Fall of Robespierre*, published in the autumn of 1794. In a pamphlet written during the following year he discusses the character of Robespierre as an 'enthusiast' in further detail:

> The Girondists, who were the first republicans in power, were men of enlarged views and great literary attainments; but they seem to have been deficient in that vigour and daring activity, which circumstances made necessary. Men of genius are rarely either prompt in action or consistent in general conduct: their early habits have been those of contemplative indolence; and the day-dreams, with which they have been accustomed to amuse their solitude, adapt them for splendid speculation, not temperate and practicable counsels. Brissot, the leader of the Gironde party, is entitled to the character of a virtuous man, and an eloquent speaker; but he was rather a sublime vision-ary, than a quick-eyed politician; and his excellences equally with his faults rendered him unfit for the helm, in the stormy hour of the Revolution. Robespierre, who displaced him, possessed a glowing ardor that still remembered the *end*, and a cool ferocity that never either overlooked, or scrupled, the *means*. What that *end* was, is not known: that it was a wicked one, has by no means been proved. I rather think, that the distant prospect to which he was travelling, appeared to him grand and beautiful; but that he fixed his eye on it with such intense eagerness as to neglect the

foulness of the road. If however his first intentions were pure, his subsequent enormities yield us a melancholy proof, that it is not the character of the possessor which directs the power, but the power which shapes and depraves the character of the possessor. In Robespierre, its influence was assisted by the properties of his disposition. – Enthusiasm, even in the gentlest temper, will frequently generate sensations of an unkindly order. If we clearly perceive any one thing to be of vast and infinite importance to ourselves and all mankind, our first feelings impel us to turn with angry contempt from those, who doubt and oppose it. The ardor of undisciplined benevolence seduces us into malignity: and whenever our hearts are warm, and our objects great and excellent, intolerance is the sin that does most easily beset us. But this enthusiasm in Robespierre was blended with gloom, and suspiciousness, and inordinate vanity. His dark imagination was still brooding over supposed plots against freedom – to prevent tyranny he became a Tyrant – and having realized the evils which he suspected, a wild and dreadful Tyrant. – Those loud-tongued adulators, the mob, overpowered the lone-whispered denunciations of conscience – he despotized in all the pomp of Patriotism, and masqueraded on the bloody stage of Revolution, a Caligula with the cap of Liberty on his head.

'Conciones ad Populum: Introductory Address',
Lectures 1795: On Politics and Religion,
eds Lewis Patton and Peter Mann (1971), pp.34–35.

To describe the poets Blake, Wordsworth, Coleridge and Southey in England or Burns in Scotland as themselves 'enthusiasts' for the ideals of the French Revolution in its early days is therefore strictly appropriate – even if, like Coleridge himself, they were more inclined towards the 'contemplative indolence' attributed to the Girondins than the 'cool ferocity' of the Jacobins. Many of those caught up in the initial fervour experienced it as something akin to divine possession – just as its opponents felt it to be more like demonic possession, and the reaction, when it came, was the more bitter. Towards the end of his life Coleridge was to warn in his *Aids to Reflection* of those who in a condition of 'enthusiasm' would 'by an uneasy and self-doubting state of mind' try to impose their particular faith on mankind generally; such people were 'fanatics' who 'in certain states of the public mind' were a menace to society. As we have seen, though Blake refused to wear his revolutionary bonnet and white cockade after the September Massacres in 1792, he never wrote against the Revolution. For all the other Romantic poets there was some kind of recantation: for Coleridge, Southey and Wordsworth it would mean eventually embracing the principles of aristocratic government and the political status quo while seeking rather to change the inner nature of humanity; for Burns a continued political radicalism combined with a no less violent detestation of its French versions.

William Godwin

William Godwin (1756–1836) was the son of a nonconformist minister and had himself trained for the ministry before becoming for a time an atheist and finally, under the influence of Coleridge, reaching again some kind of theistic position. In 1797 he married Mary Wollstonecraft, already a well-known figure as the author of *The Rights of Women* (1792), who died giving birth to their daughter, Mary, the future wife of Shelley and the author of *Frankenstein*. His stepdaughter from his second marriage, Claire Clairmont, was to have an affair with Byron and bear him a daughter, Allegra. After resigning his ministry in 1782 he lived mostly by writing – novels and even political propaganda for the Whigs during the 1780s, and later children's books (under the penname of Baldwin) and plays as well. Though in 1805 he started his own publishing house which had a big initial success with Lamb's *Tales from Shakespeare*, none of Godwin's many literary attempts brought in much money and he was constantly borrowing money, in particular from Wedgwood (the pottery manufacturer) and from his son-in-law, Shelley.

It was said by many, including Godwin himself, that the main reason why he was not prosecuted by the Pitt government was that the price of his principal political work, the *Enquiry Concerning Political Justice, and its Influence on Morals and Happiness* (1793) (36 shillings for the first edition, and 14 shillings for the subsequent ones) put it well out of the reach of the radical working-class, but it is also true that it was unlikely to have popular appeal anyway. The widest circulation of his ideas was in fact achieved through Shelley's notes to *Queen Mab*, published twenty years later, which effectively popularised the ideas of both Godwin and Holbach. Certainly in his own writing Godwin could hardly be accused of enthusiasm in any form. In spite of (or perhaps because of) the fact that it purports to deal with political emotions, *Political Justice* is an extraordinarily dry and dispassionate book. Perhaps, as Marilyn Butler has argued, this is part of a deliberate response to the calculated emotionalism and irrationality of Burke; perhaps rather, as Björn Tysdahl, a recent critic of his novels, has suggested, this very distancing from the passions so freely engendered by the Revolution in others is itself a mark of the degree to which he was haunted by unresolvable emotional tensions in his own life. Whatever the reason or reasons, the result is in startling contrast to the tone of most of the other participants in the debate. He embraces the new meaning of 'revolution' philosophically as a part of what must now be seen as a natural order of things, given the state of human passions:

> Revolution is engendered by an indignation against tyranny, yet it is itself evermore pregnant with tyranny. The tyranny which excites its indignation, can scarcely be without its partisans; and, the greater is the indignation excited, and the more sudden and vast the fall of the oppressors, the deeper will be the resentment which fills the minds of the losing party.
>
> *Political Justice*, Bk IV, Ch. 2, p.267.

The September Massacres and the growing tyranny of the Revolutionary regime are therefore to be expected. In defending the massacres as a normal part of revolution, Godwin resorts to an argument that he had employed in an earlier chapter: that human lives cannot be assumed to be of equal worth. Nothing conveys better the dispassionate tone of his arguments in *Political Justice* than his illustration concerning Fénelon, the famous and much-admired Archbishop of Cambrai:

> In a loose and general view I and my neighbour are both of us men; and of consequence entitled to equal attention. But, in reality, it is probable that one of us is a being of more worth and importance than the other. A man is of more worth than a beast; because, being possessed of higher faculties, he is capable of a more refined and genuine happiness. In the same manner the illustrious archbishop of Cambray was of more worth than his valet, and there are few of us that would hesitate to pronounce, if his palace were in flames, and the life of only one of them could be preserved, which of the two ought to be preferred.
>
> Ibid., Bk II, Ch. 2, pp.126–27.

This would still be true, he maintains, even if the valet happened to be one's father. A similar detached balancing of values, undisturbed by irrelevant emotions, should guide one's judgement of life and death on the larger political scene:

> Perhaps no important revolution was ever bloodless. It may be useful in this place, to recollect in what the mischief of shedding blood consists. The abuses which at present exist in political society are so enormous, the oppressions which are exercised so intolerable, the ignorance and vice they entail so dreadful, that possibly a dispassionate enquirer might decide that, if their annihilation could be purchased, by an instant sweeping of every human being now arrived at years of maturity, from the face of the earth, the purchase would not be too dear. It is not because human life is of so considerable value, that we ought to recoil from

the shedding of blood. Alas! the men that now exist, are for the most part poor and scanty in their portion of enjoyment, and their dignity is no more than a name. Death is in itself among the slightest of human evils. An earthquake, which should swallow up a hundred thousand individuals at once, would chiefly be to be regretted for the anguish it entailed upon survivors; in a fair estimate of those it destroyed, it would often be comparatively a trivial event. The laws of nature which produce it, are a fit subject of investigation; but their effects, contrasted with many other events, are scarcely a topic of regret. The case is altogether different, when man falls by the hand of his neighbour. Here a thousand ill passions are generated. The perpetrators, and the witnesses of murders, become obdurate, unrelenting, and inhuman. Those who sustain the loss of relations or friends by a catastrophe of this sort, are filled with indignation and revenge. Distrust is propagated from man to man, and the dearest ties of human society are dissolved. It is impossible to devise a temper, more inauspicious to the cultivation of justice, and the diffusion of benevolence.

Ibid., Bk IV, Ch. 2, pp.271–72.

Hence revolutions are bad not because they provoke massacres *per se*, but because the massacres they provoke in the nature of things engender passions that inhibit true justice. Besides, they are quite unnecessary. 'Politics,' he states with complete confidence, 'is a science.'

Imperfect institutions . . . cannot long support themselves, when they are generally disapproved of, and their effects truly understood. There is a period, at which they may be expected to decline and expire, almost without an effort. . . . When such a crisis has arrived, not a sword will need to be drawn, not a finger to be lifted up in purposes of violence. The adversaries will be too few and too feeble, to be able to entertain a serious thought of resistance against the universal sense of mankind.

Under this view of the subject then it appears, that revolutions, instead of being truly beneficial to mankind, answer no other purpose, than that of marring the salutary and uninterrupted progress, which might be expected to attend upon political truth and social improvement. They disturb the harmony of intellectual nature. They propose to give us something, for which we are not prepared, and which we cannot effectually use. They suspend the wholesome advancement of science, and confound the process of nature and reason.

Ibid., Bk IV, Ch. 2, p.274.

Samuel Taylor Coleridge

Samuel Taylor Coleridge (1772–1834) was one of the most brilliant, prolific and polymathic writers of his generation. Now remembered chiefly as the author of a handful of poems including some of the greatest in the English language ('Frost at Midnight', 'Kubla Khan' and, of course, 'The Ancient Mariner'), he was better known in his own time as a journalist, playwright, theologian, philosopher and political theorist. With Wordsworth and his close friend and brother-in-law Robert Southey he had shared the prevailing liberal enthusiasm for the Revolution in the early 1790s and at one stage had planned to emigrate to Pennsylvania (still regarded by many English at this period as being the natural home of democratic liberties) with Southey and some other friends to form an agrarian commune which they called a 'Pantisocracy'.

With the collapse of that ideal, chiefly owing to lack of money, Coleridge turned to poetry and political journalism and in the period 1795–96 gave several series of lectures on the situation in France and England and for a time during 1796 produced his own radical journal called *The Watchman*. The first extract is from a talk given in Bristol early in 1795 and simply entitled *A Moral and Political Lecture*:

The Example of France is indeed a 'Warning to Britain.' A nation wading to their Rights through Blood, and marking the track of Freedom by Devastation! Yet let us not embattle our Feelings against our Reason. Let us not indulge our malignant Passions under the mask of Humanity. Instead of railing with infuriate declamation against these excesses, we shall be more profitably employed in developing the sources of them. French Freedom is the Beacon, that while it guides us to Equality should shew us the Dangers, that throng the road.

The annals of the French Revolution have recorded in Letters of Blood, that the Knowledge of the Few cannot counteract the Ignorance of the Many; that the Light of Philosophy, when it is confined to a small Minority, points out the Possessors as the Victims, rather than the Illuminators, of the Multitude. The Patriots of France either hastened into the dangerous and gigantic Error of making certain Evil the means of contingent Good, or were sacrificed by the Mob, with whose prejudices and ferocity their unbending Virtue forbade them to assimilate. Like Sampson, the People were strong – like Sampson, the People were blind.

Lectures 1795, p.6.

Coleridge is very conscious of the new meaning that the events in France have given to the word 'revolution'; and he asks the question why such a potentially liberating experience should have gone so badly wrong. In keeping with his interest in the political psychology behind such a dramatic shift in semantics he attempts to classify the various groups advocating revolutionary social change:

There was not a Tyrant in Europe, that did not tremble on his Throne. Freedom herself heard the Crash aghast – yet shall she not have heard it unbenefited, if haply the Horrors of that Day shall have made other nations timely wise – if a great people shall from hence become adequately illuminated for a Revolution bloodless, like Poland's, but not, like Poland's, assassinated by the foul Treason of Tyrants against Liberty.

Revolutions are sudden to the unthinking only. Political Disturbances happen not without their warning Harbingers. Strange Rumblings and confused Noises still precede these earthquakes and hurricanes of the moral World. In the eventful years previous to a Revolution, the Philosopher as he passes up and down the walks of Life, examines with an anxious eye the motives and manners, that characterise those who seem destined to be the Actors in it. To delineate with a free hand the different Classes of our present Oppositionists to 'Things as they are,' – may be a delicate, but it is a necessary Task – in order that we may enlighten, or at least beware of, the misguided men who have enlisted themselves under the banners of Freedom. . . .

The first Class among the professed Friends of Liberty is composed of Men, who unaccustomed to the labor of thorough Investigation and not particularly oppressed by the Burthen of State, are yet impelled by their feelings to disapprove of its grosser depravities, and prepared to give an indolent Vote in favour of Reform. Their sensibilities unbraced by the co-operation of fixed principles, they offer no sacrifices to the divinity of active Virtue. Their political Opinions depend with weather-cock uncertainty on the winds of Rumor, that blow from France. On the report of French Victories they blaze into Republicanism, at a tale of French Excesses they darken into Aristocrats; and seek for shelter among those despicable adherents to Fraud and Tyranny, who ironically style themselves Constitutionalists. These *dough-baked Patriots* may not however be without their use. This Oscillation of political Opinion, while it retards the Day of Revolution, may operate as a preventative to its Excesses. Indecision of Character, thought the effect of Timidity, is almost always associated with benevolence.

Ibid., pp.7–9.

In contrast with these political wimps are the natural hot-heads, fired by enthusiasm unbalanced by any kind of coherent social philosophy and prepared to use violence to achieve their hazily conceived ends:

> Wilder Features characterize the second Class. Sufficiently possessed of natural Sense, to despise the Priest, and of natural Feeling to hate the Oppressor, they listen only to the inflammatory harangues of some mad-headed Enthusiast, and imbibe from them Poison, not Food, Rage not Liberty. Unillumined by Philosophy and stimulated to a lust of Revenge by aggravated wrongs, they would make the Altar of Freedom stream with blood, while the grass grew in the desolated Halls of Justice. These men are the rude Materials from which a detestable Minister manufactures Conspiracies.
>
> Ibid., p.9.

The next group is more motivated by self-interest and jealousy than by any abstract ideals of justice:

> There are a third class among the friends of Freedom who possess not the wavering character of the first description, nor the ferocity last delineated. They pursue the interests of Freedom steadily, but with narrow and self-centering views: they anticipate with exultation the abolition of privileged orders, and acts that persecute by exclusion from the rights of citizenship: they are prepared to join in digging up the rubbish of mouldering establishments and stripping off the tawdry pageantry of Governments. Whatever is above them they are most willing to drag down; but alas! they use not the pulley! Whatever tends to improve and elevate the ranks of our poorer brethren, they regard with suspicious jealousy, as the dreams of a visionary . . .
>
> Ibid., p.11.

Only a tiny minority of revolutionary sympathisers can be

classed as what Coleridge calls 'thinking and disinterested patriots' who have at once the political and philosophic vision of how the good society should order its affairs and the emotional temperament necessary to achieve that end without resorting to violence. Though he is suitably vague about how this enlightened minority must proceed, clearly Coleridge is thinking here of himself and his circle of pantisocratic friends, for this passage is followed almost at once by an extensive quotation from Southey (see p.135).

Even though out of sympathy with the course the Revolution had now taken, Coleridge, like many of his contemporaries, continued to attack the war with France, not only because it tended to make the revolutionaries in France more extreme, but also because it was counterproductive even to the declared war aims of the British themselves. Like many others, Coleridge became increasingly convinced that the real purpose of the war was not to defeat the French Revolutionary government, still less to restore the deposed Bourbons, but to distract attention from domestic problems and to permit a greater degree of repression at home (in the name of the national emergency) than would have been possible in peace time. In one of the most telling passages of *The Watchman*, in March 1796, he simply listed the objects and the achievements of the war in two parallel columns side by side:

THE WAR

ITS OBJECTS	OBTAINED
December 1792	
To prevent the Opening of the Scheldt,	By its being solemnly opened.
To save Holland,	By its being conquered.
To prevent the aggrandizement of France,	By France conquering territories almost equal in extent to her own.

June 1793

Indemnity for the past,	Martinico, Pondicherry, and Corsica, gained at an expence of Sixty Millions sterling, being more than twenty times their value.
Security for the future,	In making France an armed nation, and the greatest military power in Europe.
Gratitude to our Allies.	Most of whom have taken our money and left us in the lurch, and the others only fight with us as long as we can pay them.

October 1793

The Restoration of Monarchy in France,	By establishing a Republic, and seeing those who voted the death of Louis the XVIth appointed to the supreme Government of France.
The Renunciation of the system of Fraternity,	By the French consolidating the Netherlands, Savoy, &c. and even wishing to consolidate a great part of Germany with their Republic.
The destruction of Jacobin principles,	By the appointment of Jacobins to fill the Offices of Government.

February 1795

That France should have a Government capable of maintaining the accustomed Relations of Peace and Amity with other Powers.	France never was without such a Govern-ment. She observed the Relations of Peace and Amity with Sweden, Denmark, Switzerland, America, &c.

29 October 1795

Till the stability of the New Constitution is proved,	And it was *fully* proved in less than six weeks, namely, on the 8th of December, 1795.

March 1796

God knows the object of the War!	God knows whether it is obtained.

The Watchman, ed. Lewis Patton (1970), pp.108–9.

William Wordsworth

William Wordsworth (1770–1850) was more closely involved with the Revolution than any other contemporary poet. In spite of considerable poverty in his early life, he had received a good education at Hawkshead Grammar School (then one of the best schools in the north of England) under conditions of peculiar liberty. He was permitted, for instance, to stay out all night walking by himself in the Lake District fells – something sanctioned by few boarding-systems then or now. It also gave him an abiding sense of the equality of man and the fraternity of the intellect:

> For, born in a poor District, and which yet
> Retaineth more of ancient homeliness,
> Manners erect, and frank simplicity,

Than any other nook of English Land,
It was my fortune scarcely to have seen
Through the whole tenor of my schoolday time
The face of one, who, whether boy or man,
Was vested with attention or respect
Through claims of wealth or blood. Nor was it least
Of many debts which afterwards I owed
To Cambridge and an academic life,
That something there was holden up to view
Of a republic, where all stood thus far
Upon equal ground, that they were brothers all
In honour, as of one community –
Scholars and gentlemen – where, furthermore,
Distinction lay open to all that came,
And wealth and titles were in less esteem
Than talents and successful industry.

Prelude (1805), Bk IX, ll.218–36.

Like so many other graduates of the period who lacked family money or good connections, he left Cambridge resigned to becoming an Anglican clergyman, but before seeking ordination he visited France in 1791 with the idea of perfecting his French and possibly finding alternative and more congenial employment as a tutor to some aristocratic family. It was there, while staying in the city of Orleans, that he met briefly two people who were to be among the most influential figures in his life. The first was Michel Armand Beaupuy (1755–96), mentioned above, a republican officer in the then still strongly royalist army, who transformed Wordsworth's attitude to the Revolution from one of sentimental interest to passionate commitment. Most of his fellow-officers identified themselves with the aristocracy and were deeply hostile to the Revolution:

A knot of military Officers,
That to a Regiment appertain'd which then
Was station'd in the City, were the chief
Of my associates: some of these wore Swords
Which had been seasoned in the Wars, and all
Were men well born, at least laid claim to such

Distinction, as the Chivalry of France.
In age and temper differing, they had yet
One spirit ruling in them all, alike
(Save only one, hereafter to be nam'd)
Were bent upon undoing what was done:
This was their rest, and only hope, therewith
No fear had they of bad becoming worse,
For worst to them was come, nor would have stirr'd,
Or deem'd it worth a moment's while to stir,
In anything, save only as the act
Look'd thitherward.

Ibid., Bk IX, ll.126–42.

In its initial stages the French Revolution had been a largely Parisian affair and the provinces, though now involved, were much more deeply divided and less under the control of the central government. In the most conservative area, La Vendée, there was even a pro-monarchist revolt. The disaffected royalist officers in Orleans awaited only the moment to take part in a counter-coup or to join the Prussian and Austrian armies mustering with French *émigré* forces on the French borders at Coblenz to march on Paris and restore the Bourbon monarchy. In this they were not alone: by April 1792 more than half the 9,000 or so officers of the French army had deserted to join the royalist forces:

        . . . 'Twas in truth an hour
Of universal ferment – mildest men
Were agitated, and commotions, strife
Of passion and opinion filled the walls
Of peaceful houses with unquiet sounds.
The soil of common life was at that time
Too hot to tread upon. Oft said I then,
And not then only, 'What a mockery this
Of history, the past and that to come!
Now do I feel how I have been deceived,
Reading of Nations and their works in faith –
Faith given to vanity and emptiness –
Oh, laughter for the page that would reflect

To future times the face of what now is!'
The land all swarmed with passion, like a plain
Devoured by locusts – Carra, Gorsas – add
A hundred other names, forgotten now,
Nor to be heard of more, yet were they powers,
Like earthquakes, shocks repeated day by day,
And felt through every nook of town and field.

The Men already spoken of as chief
Of my associates were prepared for flight
To augment the band of emigrants in arms
Upon the borders of the Rhine, and leagued
With foreign foes mustered for instant war.
This was their undisguised intent, and they
Were waiting with the whole of their desires
The moment to depart.

Ibid., ll.164–90.

Gorsas and Carra were two journalists, deputies of the National Assembly who were associated with the Girondin party, later to be purged by their rivals, the Jacobins, in the Reign of Terror during 1793. Wordsworth seems to have told Carlyle later that he had been present at Gorsas' execution – in which case, it has been conjectured, he must have made a brief return trip to Paris late in 1793.

This circle of royalist officers would, however, have been equally hostile to Girondins and Jacobins alike, and Beaupuy's pro-Revolutionary enthusiasm was all the more remarkable and moving to the young and impressionable Wordsworth. Not surprisingly perhaps, such a 'patriot', in the new republican sense that the word had taken on with the threat of invasion by the combined royalist forces, was rejected by his fellows with what Wordsworth vividly calls 'an oriental loathing' for belonging to 'a different cast(e)' – a political untouchable. Perhaps partly because he was such an outcast, he became a close companion of the young English poet on long walks across the French countryside. On one such occasion an incident occurred which for Wordsworth came to epitomise all the organised injustice and privilege of the *ancien régime*:

> . . .We chanced
> One day to meet a hunger-bitten girl,
> Who crept along, fitting her languid self
> Unto a heifer's motion – by a cord
> Tied to her arm, and picking thus from the lane
> Its sustenance, while the girl with her two hands
> Was busy knitting in a heartless mood
> Of solitude – and at the sight my friend
> In agitation said, ''Tis against *that*
> Which we are fighting,' I with him believed
> Devoutly that a spirit was abroad
> Which could not be withstood, that poverty
> At least like this, would in a little time
> Be found no more, that we should see the earth
> Unthwarted in her wish to recompense
> The industrious, and the lowly child of toil,
> All institutes for ever blotted out
> That legalised exclusion, empty pomp
> Abolished, sensual state and cruel power
> Whether by edict of the one or few –
> And finally, as sum and crown of all,
> Should see the people having a strong hand
> In making their own laws, whence better days
> To all mankind.

Ibid., ll.511–34.

Beaupuy subsequently became Chief of Staff in the Republican army during the civil war in the Vendée, and was later killed at Emmendingen, on the eastern front, in 1796.

The other meeting that was to change the course of Wordsworth's life was with Annette Vallon, the daughter of a surgeon of strict Catholic and royalist background from the provincial town of Blois, whom Wordsworth met in January 1792. They fell passionately in love, but their marriage was strongly opposed by her family on both political and religious grounds. Nevertheless, possibly in an effort to force the family's hand, in the spring of that year she became pregnant; the family intervened and the lovers were forced to separate. By the time their daughter Caroline was born in Orleans in

December 1792 the political situation was rapidly worsening. With massacres at home and the threat of foreign invasion the Revolution had lost its original mood of internationalism and foreigners (especially Englishmen who had been known to consort with counter-revolutionary officers in the army) were increasingly suspect. Wordsworth himself, who had never been well off, was by now almost out of money. He returned to Paris in the autumn of that year and thence to England just before the outbreak of war between the two countries early in 1793 in a mood bordering on despair – separated from the woman he loved and their child; disillusioned with the new dawn for mankind he had hoped for with the Revolution, but even more so with his own country for its determined opposition to the Revolution in which, for all its excesses, he still passionately believed.

Wordsworth arrived in Paris sometime in October 1792 in the aftermath of the September Massacres, torn between optimism and forebodings for the future:

> This was the time in which, enflamed with hope,
> To Paris I returned. Again I ranged
> More eagerly than I had done before
> Through the wide city, and in progress passed
> The prison where the unhappy monarch lay,
> Associate with his children and his wife
> In bondage, and the palace, lately stormed
> With roar of cannon and a numerous host.
> I crossed – a black and empty area then –
> The square of the Carousel, few weeks back
> Heaped up with dead and dying, upon these
> And other sights looking as doth a man
> Upon a volume whose contents he knows
> Are memorable but from him locked up,
> Being written in a tongue he cannot read,
> So that he questions the mute leaves with pain,
> And half upbraids their silence. But that night
> When on my bed I lay, I was most moved
> And felt most deeply in what world I was;
> My room was high and lonely, near the roof
> Of a large mansion or hotel, a spot

That would have pleased me in more quiet times –
Nor was it wholly without pleasure then.
With unextinguished taper I kept watch,
Reading at intervals. The fear gone by
Pressed on me almost like a fear to come.
I thought of those September massacres,
Divided from me by a little month,
And felt and touched them, a substantial dread
(The rest was conjured up from tragic fictions,
And mournful calendars of true history,
Remembrances and dim admonishments):
'The horse is taught his manage, and the wind
Of heaven wheels round and treads in his own steps,
Year follows year, the tide returns again,
Day follows day, all things have second birth;
The earthquake is not satisfied at once' –
And in such way I wrought upon myself,
Until I seemed to hear a voice that cried
To the whole city, 'Sleep no more!'

Ibid., Bk X, ll.38–77.

Though he makes a veiled allusion to his love-affair with Annette in the story of Vaudracour and Julia (Ibid., Bk IX, ll.556–935) – which fictionalised account ends on a note of even deeper dejection, he describes his own mood at this stage purely in terms of his political hopes and fears, suggesting that, had he stayed, he might well have died fighting for the Revolution:

       . . . In this frame of mind
Reluctantly to England I returned,
Compelled by nothing less than absolute want
Of funds for my support; else, well assured
That I both was and must be of small worth,
No better than an alien in the land,
I doubtless should have made a common cause
With some who perished, haply perished too –
A poor mistaken and bewildered offering,
Should to the breast of Nature have gone back,

> With all my resolutions, all my hopes,
> A poet only to myself, to men
> Useless. . . .

Ibid., ll.188–200.

Wordsworth was a passionately patriotic man, and though he could no longer see in the Revolution what it had once seemed to promise, he was convinced that the British quarrel with France was both unjust and likely only to make the Revolution more extreme in its violence at home and anti-foreign in its outlook. His suggestion that he might have stayed and fought for the Revolution shows just how passionate his feelings were. To have considered fighting for France was to have considered actually taking up arms against his own country. It is interesting to notice how he applies the word 'revolution' to his own feelings at this stage in a kind of internalisation of the new, post-Burkeian, meaning to the word which he had experienced at first-hand. Wordsworth describes his alienated state on his return to England in words that closely echo those of the ending of 'The Ancient Mariner' in the poem he and Coleridge had begun to write as a joint venture and which was to lead to the writing of the *Lyrical Ballads* shortly before he wrote this part of *The Prelude*:

> And now the strength of Britain was put forth
> In league with the confederated host;
> Not in my single self alone I found,
> But in the minds of all ingenuous youth,
> Change and subversion from this hour. No shock
> Given to my moral nature had I known
> Down to that very moment – neither lapse
> Nor turn of sentiment – that might be named
> A revolution, save at this one time:
> All else was progress on the self-same path
> On which with a diversity of pace
> I had been travelling; this, a stride at once
> Into another region. True it is,
> 'Twas not concealed with what ungracious eyes
> Our native rulers from the very first

Had looked upon regenerated France;
Nor had I doubted that this day would come –
But in such contemplation I had thought
Of general interests only, beyond this
Had never once foretasted the event.
Now had I other business, for I felt
The ravage of this most unnatural strife
In my own heart; there lay it like a weight,
At enmity with all the tenderest springs
Of my enjoyments. I, who with the breeze
Had played, a green leaf on the blessed tree
Of my beloved country – nor had wished
For happier fortune than to wither there,
Now from my pleasant station was cut off,
And tossed about in whirlwinds. I rejoiced,
Yes, afterwards, truth painful to record,
Exulted in the triumph of my soul
When Englishmen by thousands were o'erthrown,
Left without glory on the field, or driven,
Brave hearts, to shameful flight. It was a grief –
Grief call it not, 'twas any thing but that –
A conflict of sensations without name,
Of which he only who may love the sight
Of a village steeple as I do can judge,
When in the congregation, bending all
To their great Father, prayers were offered up,
Or praises for our country's victories,
And, 'mid the simple worshippers perchance
I only, like an uninvited guest
Whom no one owned, sate silent – shall I add,
Fed on the day of vengeance yet to come!

Ibid., Bk X, ll.229–74.

In retrospect Wordsworth came to see that spiritual and moral
crisis over the Revolution and his attitude both to it and to
his own country as being the foundation of his mature growth
as a poet. It is significant that, having completed the *Lyrical
Ballads* in collaboration with Coleridge, his next act was to
begin work on the enormous autobiographical poem we now

know as *The Prelude*, but which he always thought of as 'the poem to Coleridge'. It was never published in his lifetime, though fragments were cut out to form a number of shorter poems, and he continued to revise and alter it over a period of 40 years. There is, as a result, not so much a single stable authoritative text as a series of texts forming an on-going process in his mind, and he writes and rewrites his story obsessively at the various stages of his life to make sense of what happened to him in particular during those few dramatic years in the early 1790s. Our quotations have all been from the 1805 text, which gives a rather different perspective on the Revolution from that of the final text published only after his death in 1850. In particular the 1805 text seems in certain ways to have been modelled on one of the most famous spiritual autobiographies of all time, St Augustine's *Confessions*: both are divided into thirteen books, and where for Augustine the crisis occurs with his conversion to Christianity, Wordsworth, in what seems to be a deliberate parallel, places his crisis over the French Revolution.

>   Thus I fared,
> Dragging all passions, notions, shapes of faith,
> Like culprits to the bar, suspiciously
> Calling the mind to establish in plain day
> Her titles and her honours, now believing,
> Now disbelieving, endlessly perplexed
> With impulse, motive, right and wrong, the ground
> Of moral obligation – what the rule
> And what the sanction – till, demanding proof,
> And seeking it in every thing, I lost
> All feeling of conviction, and, in fine,
> Sick, wearied out with contrarieties,
> Yielded up moral questions in despair,
> And for my future studies, as the sole
> Employment of the enquiring faculty,
> Turned towards mathematics, and their clear
> And solid evidence.
>   Ah! then it was
> That thou, most precious friend, about this time
> First known to me, didst lend a living help

To regulate my soul. And then it was
That the beloved woman in whose sight
Those days were passed – now speaking in a voice
Of sudden admonition like a brook
That does but cross a lonely road; and now
Seen, heard and felt, and caught at every turn,
Companion never lost through many a league –
Maintained for me a saving intercourse
With my true self (for, though impaired, and changed
Much, as it seemed, I was no further changed
Than as a clouded, not a waning moon);
She, in the midst of all, preserved me still
A poet, made me seek beneath that name
My office upon earth, and nowhere else.
And lastly, Nature's self, by human love
Assisted, through the weary labyrinth
Conducted me again to open day,
Revived the feelings of my earlier life,
Gave me that strength and knowledge full of peace,
Enlarged, and never more to be disturbed,
Which through the steps of our degeneracy,
All degradation of this age, hath still
Upheld me, and upholds me at this day
In the catastrophe (for so they dream,
And nothing less), when, finally to close
And rivet up the gains of France, a Pope
Is summoned in to crown an Emperor –
This last opprobrium, when we see the dog
Returning to his vomit, when the sun
That rose in splendour, was alive, and moved
In exultation among living clouds,
Hath put his function and his glory off,
And, turned into a gewgaw, a machine,
Sets like an opera phantom.

Ibid., Bk X, ll.888–940.

The crowning of Napoleon as Emperor by the Pope in 1804
is, for Wordsworth, the ultimate obscenity and final extinction
of his revolutionary faith: 'the dog returning to its vomit'. It

also marked the end of any lingering sympathy he may have felt for the French cause. In *The Convention of Cintra* (1809) he declares that until the invasion and subjugation of Switzerland by Napoleon's forces in 1797 the mass of the British people were still 'on the side of their nominal enemies'. With the French invasion of Portugal and Spain in 1807–8 and the outbreak of the Peninsular War the moral balance was finally reversed. Napoleonic France was now the oppressor, Britain the champion of freedom and liberty. But in that process Wordsworth had also irrevocably lost his faith in the power of politics to serve human liberty. Henceforth his enthusiasms were reserved largely for individuals and solitary figures relating more to the unchanging permanencies of nature than to the fickle and transient moods of the urban mob, whether French or English.

Robert Burns

Robert Burns (1759–96) shares with Blake the distinction of being one of the two major Romantic poets not to come from a middle or upper-class and university background. This does not mean that he was ill-educated, however, any more than Blake was. Though his father was an impoverished Ayrshire tenant farmer, the family was literate and the young Burns had access to the major English classics. When he was lionised by the Edinburgh society of the day, he was well able to hold his own in literary conversation and was noted for his brilliance and wit. Nevertheless, throughout his life he was plagued by the ambiguities of his social status. There was in Scotland no equivalent to the relatively classless circle in London that centred on the house of Joseph Johnson. If he was acceptable as a poet and Scottish celebrity, he was also always made conscious that his relationship with his literary peers and associates was not one between equals. He, in return, stressed his own peasant origins, and his use of the vernacular in much of his best poetry (he could, and did, of course, also write in standard English) is as much an ideological as an aesthetic choice.

Having tried his hand at farming, Burns, like Paine, settled in the unlikely profession of an Excise (customs) officer. In February 1792 he led the boarding party on to a smugglers' schooner, the *Rosamund*, which had gone aground in the Solway Firth. It is said that he himself afterwards bought three of the ship's guns and had them sent to France to show his sympathy with the Revolutionary government there. Certainly in December that year there was an official enquiry into his loyalty and he was forced to make a formal recantation of his republican views. With the declaration of war two months later Burns' patriotism seems to have finally overcome his enthusiasm for the Revolution, which was already waning as France showed 'her old avidity for conquest, in annexing Savoy, &c. to her dominions, & invading the rights of Holland'. Nevertheless, his burning sense of the injustice inherent in the social stratification and the unequal distribution of wealth of the day remained undiminished, and in 1794 he wrote perhaps his most famous attack on wealth and privilege:

Is there for honest poverty,
  That hings his head, an' a' that?
The coward slave, we pass him by –
  We dare be poor for a' that!
For a' that, an' a' that,
  Our toils obscure, an' a' that,
The rank is but the guinea's stamp;
  The man's the gowd for a' that.

What though on hamely fare we dine,
  Wear hoddin grey an' a' that?
Gie fools their silks, and knaves their wine –
  A man's a man for a' that!
For a' that, an' a' that,
  Their tinsel show, an' a' that,
The honest man, tho' e'er sae poor,
  Is king o'men for a' that.

Ye see yon birkie, ca'd 'a lord,'
  Wha struts, an' stares, an' a' that?
Tho' hundreds worship at his word,
  He's but a cuif for a' that:

For a' that, an' a' that,
His ribband, star, an' a' that,
The man o'independent mind,
He looks an' laughs at a' that.

A prince can mak a belted knight,
A marquis, duke, an' a' that;
But an honest man's aboon his might –
Guid faith, he mauna fa' that!
For a' that, an' a' that,
Their dignities, an' a' that,
The pith o'sense, an' pride o'worth,
Are higher rank than a' that.

Then let us pray that come it may,
As come it will for a' that,
That Sense and Worth, o'er a' the earth,
Shall bear the gree an' a' that;
For a' that, an' a' that,
It's comin yet for a' that,
That man to man, the world o'er,
Shall brithers be for a' that!

Robert Southey

Robert Southey (1774–1843) is the third member of the great triumvirate of Lake poets. Coleridge's closest friend in the Pantisocratic days before meeting Wordsworth, Southey became his brother-in-law, and for much of his later life the sole financial support of Mrs Coleridge and her children who lived with the Southeys at Greta Hall, Keswick, after her separation from her drug-addicted husband. At the time he was commonly considered at least the equal of Coleridge and Wordsworth as a poet, but little of his work beyond a few anthology-pieces is read today.

Like them he was an enthusiast for the Revolution in its early days. 'Few persons,' he wrote later, 'but those who have lived in it can conceive or comprehend what the memory of the French Revolution was, nor what a visionary world seemed to open upon those who were just entering it. Old things seemed passing away, and nothing was dreamt of but the regeneration of the human race.' While still at Westminster School he gave vent to his radicalism through a newsheet entitled *The Flagellant* which he started with a group of friends. The fifth issue contained an article by him condemning flogging which was seen as so subversive to the values of the school that he was expelled. Christ Church (College), Oxford, where he had been entered, thereupon refused to admit him, and he went to Balliol instead.

Though his poetry has not lasted well, there was, as *The Flagellant* incident showed, no doubt about his talents as a journalist and propagandist, and what was later to earn him the hatred and scorn not just of his one-time fellow radicals but even of such un-revolutionary figures as Thomas Love Peacock, was not so much his turning against the Revolution as his unforgivable act of accepting a 'pension' (i.e. a regular salary) to become a mouthpiece and apologist for the repressive actions of the British government.

In 1794, however, he was still, if not an ardent Revolutionary, at least an ardent reformist. In his *Moral and Political Lecture* of that year Coleridge includes a poem by Southey entitled *To the Exiled Patriots* which was originally intended for Daniel Isaac Eaton's *Politics for the People*. It begins:

> Martyrs of Freedom – ye who firmly good
> Stept forth the champions in her glorious cause,
> Ye who against Corruption nobly stood
> For Justice, Liberty, and equal Laws.
>
> Ye who have urged the cause of man so well
> Whilst proud Oppression's torrent swept along,
> Ye who so firmly stood, so nobly fell,
> Accept one ardent Briton's grateful song.

By far Southey's best-known poem, however, is *The Battle of Blenheim*, which is often reprinted simply as an anti-war poem. It is certainly that: but it loses much of its force, if it is not seen in its context of the anti-war agitation of the late 1790s. The Battle of Blenheim, the 'famous victory" of the poem, had been fought to check the territorial ambitions of

the French king, Louis XIV. Now, thanks to the efforts of
the British government and its allies (in effect the same coalition
that had defeated Louis), France had been transformed
from an internationalist state preaching liberty, equality and
brotherhood into a military power that under Napoleon was
well on the way to becoming an even greater threat to the
peace and stability of Europe than Louis XIV had ever been:

The Battle of Blenheim

It was a summer evening,
Old Kaspar's work was done,
And he before his cottage door
    Was sitting in the sun.
And by him sported on the green
His little grandchild Wilhelmine.

She saw her brother Peterkin
    Roll something large and round,
Which he beside the rivulet
    In playing there had found;
He came to ask what he had found,
That was so large, and smooth, and round.

Old Kaspar took it from the boy,
    Who stood expectant by;
And then the old man shook his head,
    And, with a natural sigh,
''Tis some poor fellow's skull,' said he,
'Who fell in the great victory.

'I find them in the garden,
    For there's many here about;
And often when I go to plough,
    The ploughshare turns them out!
For many thousand men,' said he,
'Were slain in that great victory.'

'Now tell us what 'twas all about,'
    Young Peterkin, he cries;
And little Wilhelmine looks up
    With wonder-waiting eyes;

'Now tell us all about the war,
And what they fought each other for.'

'It was the English,' Kaspar cried,
 'Who put the French to rout;
But what they fought each other for,
 I could not well make out;
But everybody said', quoth he,
'That 'twas a famous victory.

'My father lived at Blenheim then,
 Yon little stream hard by;
They burnt his dwelling to the ground,
 And he was forced to fly;
So with his wife and child he fled,
Nor had he where to rest his head.

'With fire and sword the country round
 Was wasted far and wide,
And many a childing mother then,
 And new-born baby died;
But things like that, you know, must be
At every famous victory.

'They say it was a shocking sight
 After the field was won;
For many thousand bodies here
 Lay rotting in the sun;
But things like that, you know, must be
At every famous victory.

'Great praise the Duke of Marlbro' won,
 And our good Prince Eugene.'
'Why 'twas a very wicked thing!'
 Said little Wilhelmine.
'Nay, nay, my little girl,' quoth he,
'It was a famous victory.

'And everybody praised the Duke
 Who this great fight did win.'
'But what good came of it at last?'
 Quoth little Peterkin.
'Why that I cannot tell,' said he,
'But 'twas a famous victory.'

PART B: THE CONDITION OF ENGLAND QUESTION

The Influence of Milton

The phrase in the title is Carlyle's; the question is one which, as we have seen, was inescapably raised by the French Revolution and, once raised, obstinately refused to go away. No disillusion with the course of events in France, no appeals to patriotism, no threat of invasion by Napoleon, no measures to censor the press, no exemplary treason-trials could in the end stem the growing sense of the British public that the corruption of the state was a flagrant scandal and that reform in almost every area of public life was long overdue.

Though by 1802 Wordsworth had lost his initial enthusiasm for the Revolution in France, he can still appeal instead to the figure who, for him, is (in the new sense of the word) the greatest of the English 'revolutionaries' from the seventeenth century:

> Milton! thou shouldst be living at this hour:
> England hath need of thee: she is a fen
> Of stagnant waters: altar, sword and pen,
> Fireside, the heroic wealth of hall and bower,
> Have forfeited their ancient English dower
> Of inward happiness. We are all selfish men;
> Oh! raise us up, return to us again;
> And give us manners, virtue, freedom, power.

Nor is Wordsworth's view exceptional among the poets. Almost a decade earlier Blake's reaction to the Revolution had been to look with new eyes upon the abuses of his own society. In 'London', for instance, the soldier, normally the hated symbol of repression, is seen as a victim of the system as much as the more obviously exploited chimneysweep; but the real climax of the hypocrisy of what might be called the 'spiritual *ancien régime*' comes in the last verse which deals with the double-standard of sexual behaviour:

I wander thro' each charter'd street,
Near where the charter'd Thames does flow,
And mark in every face I meet
Marks of weakness, marks of woe.

In every cry of every Man,
In every Infant's cry of fear,
In every voice, in every ban,
The mind-forg'd manacles I hear.

How the Chimney-sweeper's cry
Every black'ning Church appalls;
And the hapless Soldier's sigh
Runs in blood down Palace walls.

But most thro' midnight streets I hear
How the youthful Harlot's curse
Blasts the new born Infant's tear,
And blights with plagues the Marriage hearse.

Milton, we recall, was to be the subject of one of Blake's most massive later works. In harking back to Milton as the poet-hero of the earlier revolution, it would appear at first glance that Blake and Wordsworth are doing no more than add their handfuls to the mountain of praise that had been heaped on him throughout the earlier part of the century. Yet there is a profound difference. The Milton that had been adulated by earlier generations of the eighteenth century was a carefully sanitised version; Milton the religious heretic, the social, political and sexual rebel had been tacitly allowed to drop from sight. What was left was simply the lover of liberty and great 'religious poet', the author of *Paradise Lost* and *Paradise Regained*. The re-invocation of Milton after the French Revolution never lost sight of the fact that his poetry was inescapably bound up with his attack on the political and social status quo.

Thus Shelley in *Queen Mab* moves directly from a diatribe against poverty and its social effects – what today we would call 'cognitive poverty' – to an invocation of Milton. In so doing he deliberately echoes a famous reference to the possibility that the village churchyard might contain the grave of some 'mute inglorious Milton' in one of the best-known mid-eighteenth-century poems, Gray's *Elegy in a Country Churchyard*:

> Perhaps in this neglected spot is laid
> Some heart once pregnant with celestial fire;
> Hands that the rod of empire might have swayed,
> Or waked to ecstasy the living lyre.
>
> But knowledge to their eyes her ample page
> Rich with the scrolls of time did ne'er unroll;
> Chill Penury repressed their noble rage,
> And froze the genial current of the soul.
>
> . . . Some village Hampden, that with dauntless breast
> The little tyrant of his fields withstood;
> Some mute inglorious Milton here may rest,
> Some Cromwell guiltless of his country's blood.

> ll.45–60.

There is a curious acceptance about this state of affairs for Gray. It is not a divinely-appointed hierarchy that keeps the peasant in his place but simple poverty; yet there is no suggestion here that anything should be changed. *Queen Mab* deliberately recalls this passage, but Shelley's verse is alive with indignation:

> The iron rod of penury still compels
> Her wretched slave to bow the knee to wealth,
> And poison, with unprofitable toil,
> A life too void of solace to confirm
> The very chains that bind him to his doom.
> Nature, impartial in munificence,
> Has gifted man with all-subduing will:
> Matter, with all its transitory shapes,
> Lies subjected and plastic at his feet,
> That, weak from bondage, tremble as they tread.
> How many a rustic Milton has passed by,
> Stifling the speechless longings of his heart,
> In unremitting drudgery and care!

How many a vulgar Cato has compelled
His energies, no longer tameless then,
To mould a pin, or fabricate a nail!
How many a Newton, to whose passive ken
Those mighty spheres that gem infinity
Were only specks of tinsel, fixed in heaven
To light the midnights of his native town!

ll.127–46.

Percy Bysshe Shelley

To many people, then and now, the life of Percy Bysshe Shelley (1792–1822) seemed to encapsulate and typify all that might be expected of a Romantic poet. He was an aristocrat (the son of a baronet) who espoused the cause of liberty and of the people. A persecuted outsider and rebel at Eton, he was sent down from Oxford in 1810 for writing *The Necessity of Atheism*. The following year he eloped with and married the daughter of an innkeeper, Harriet Westbrook, and was promptly disowned by his family. In 1812 he went to Ireland to assist in the campaign then being waged to give the vote to Catholics, but within a few months he returned to help in the defence of Daniel Isaac Eaton – and after the latter's sentence he wrote *A Letter to Lord Ellenborough*, an impassioned plea on Eaton's behalf.

His first major poem, *Queen Mab* (1813), included an attack on the institutions of monarchy, aristocracy, religion and marriage, the economic exploitation of the poor, and war – especially the continuing war with Napoleonic France. This vision of the miseries and evils of present society was contrasted with a vision of an egalitarian and anarchist society of the future, run along more or less Godwinian lines. The following year Shelley confirmed the popular image of him as a dangerous radical and sexual libertine by abandoning Harriet (pregnant with her second child) and eloping with Mary, the daughter of Godwin and Mary Wollstonecraft – much to the anger of Godwin, whose theoretical views on free-love did not quite stretch to the behaviour of his own daughter or her married lover. Mary Shelley (as she became two and a half years later when Harriet committed suicide) was herself to become a famous author with the publication of her novel, *Frankenstein*.

In the spring of 1818 Shelley left England for Italy, where he was to remain for the rest of his short life. While there he wrote a number of poems on reform, including the Song to the Men of England, England in 1819 and, most notably, The Masque of Anarchy, inspired by the Peterloo Massacre of 1819, where a peaceful demonstration at St Peter's Fields, Manchester, that included many women and children, had been charged by troops who killed eleven of the demonstrators and injured many more. It was promptly dubbed 'Peterloo' in ironic contrast to the heroism of the army in defeating Napoleon at Waterloo only four years earlier. Shelley also began a political pamphlet, *A Philosophical View of Reform*. In July 1822 he was drowned in a storm at sea.

If Wordsworth, writing in 1802, could afford some degree of optimism by looking back to past glories, Shelley, writing seventeen years later after the conclusion of the Napoleonic Wars had seen everywhere what seemed like the triumph of despotism and in England the savage repression of Peterloo, can find no such inspiration. What hope there is must lie in the future – and it is but a very feeble ray.

ENGLAND IN 1819

An old, mad, blind, despised, and dying king, –
Princes, the dregs of their dull race, who flow
Through public scorn – mud from a muddy spring;
Rulers, who neither see, nor feel, nor know,
But leech-like to their fainting country cling,
Till they drop, blind in blood, without a blow;
A people starved and stabbed in the untilled field, –
An army, which liberticide and prey
Makes as a two-edged sword to all who wield –
Golden and sanguine laws which tempt and slay, –
Religion Christless, Godless – a book sealed;
A Senate, – Time's worst statute unrepealed, –
Are graves, from which a glorious Phantom may
Burst, to illumine our tempestuous day.

His Song to the Men of England, written as part of a projected series of poems for working men that remained unpublished at the time, is hardly more optimistic.

> Men of England, wherefore plough
> For the lords who lay ye low?
> Wherefore weave with toil and care,
> The rich robes your tyrants wear?
>
> Wherefore feed, and clothe, and save,
> From the cradle to the grave,
> Those ungrateful drones who would
> Drain your sweat – nay, drink your blood!
>
> Wherefore, Bees of England, forge
> Many a weapon, chain, and scourge,
> That these stingless drones may spoil
> The forced produce of your toil?
>
> Have ye leisure, comfort, calm,
> Shelter, food, love's gentle balm?
> Or what is it ye buy so dear
> With your pain and with your fear?
>
> The seed ye sow, another reaps;
> The wealth ye find, another keeps;
> The robes ye weave, another wears;
> The arms ye forge, another bears.
>
> Sow seed, – but let no tyrant reap;
> Find wealth, – let no impostor heap;
> Weave robes, – let not the idle wear;
> Forge arms, – in your defence to bear.
>
> Shrink to your cellars, holes, and cells;
> In halls ye deck, another dwells.
> Why shake the chains ye wrought? Ye see
> The steel ye tempered glance on ye.
>
> With plough and spade, and hoe and loom,
> Trace your grave, and build your tomb,
> And weave your winding-sheet, till fair
> England be your sepulchre.

All three are in their own ways powerful poems, yet there is a sense in which the immediate topical passion that gives them their force reduces their universal impact. Their very topicality makes them, in retrospect, period pieces. At the same time as he was at work on these, however, Shelley also produced another sonnet which, while it shares the anger and contempt for despotism that fires the other poems, sublimates it into an understated irony. It is, deservedly, one of Shelley's finest and best-known poems.

   Ozymandias is the Greek version of the name of Ramses II, a Pharaoh of Egypt in the thirteenth century B.C. According to the account of a first-century B.C. historian, Diodorus Siculus, his statue was the largest in all Egypt and bore the inscription: 'I am Ozymandias, king of kings; if anyone wishes to know what I am and where I lie, let him surpass me in some of my exploits'. The new academic science of egyptology may be said to have begun with Napoleon's Egyptian expedition in 1798, and the implicit reference to the subsequent career of Napoleon as much as to the original Pharaoh would have been obvious to any contemporary reader:

> I met a traveller from an antique land
> Who said: Two vast and trunkless legs of stone
> Stand in the desert. Near them, on the sand,
> Half sunk, a shattered visage lies, whose frown,
> And wrinkled lip, and sneer of cold command,
> Tell that its sculptor well those passions read
> Which yet survive, stamped on these lifeless things,
> The hand that mocked them, and the heart that fed;
> And on the pedestal these words appear:
> 'My name is Ozymandias, king of kings:
> Look on my works, ye Mighty, and despair!'
> Nothing beside remains. Round the decay
> Of that colossal wreck, boundless and bare,
> The lone and level sands stretch far away.

William Cobbett

William Cobbett (1763–1835) was the self-educated son of an innkeeper, who rose from ploughboy to soldier, from soldier to journalist and from journalist to Member of Parliament. For nearly 40 years he was to occupy a unique position in both Britain and America: 'no other private person', writes George Spater, his most outstanding biographer, 'before or since has had such a dominating influence on public affairs on both sides of the Atlantic'. His influence was based on his extraordinary power and facility as a writer and journalist coupled with his equally extraordinary range of experience.

From 1785–91 he served as a British soldier on the U.S.–Canadian border, living largely among loyalists who had fled northwards after the War of Independence. There he was appalled at the waste and corruption of the army, and on his return to England was eventually court-martialled for petitioning the Secretary for War about the misconduct of his officers. On discovering that vital evidence had been tampered with and that he was certain to be found guilty of 'wilfully and maliciously . . . calumniating the characters of the officers in question', he fled to France in 1792 and from there to Philadelphia where he lived until 1800. During that period he made his name as a journalist, defending both Washington's administration and British interests. On his return to England in 1800 the government welcomed him as a conservative ally, but a closer view of the condition of the country turned him into a radical reformer.

As a writer he was both loved and feared. Joseph Priestley, another victim of the anti-radical backlash against the French Revolution, who had moved to America, described him there as being 'by far the most popular writer in this country'. In 1807 the *Edinburgh Review* declared that Cobbett had more influence in England than all other journalists put together. His output was enormous: he wrote more than twenty million words, which puts him among the most voluminous writers who have ever lived. In addition to his *Weekly Political Register* and his *Rural Rides*, he wrote books and pamphlets on law, grammar, gardening, the Reformation, child-rearing and the life of the American President, Andrew Jackson.

It was once again his interference in army matters that gave the government their excuse to proceed against him. In 1809 there had been an incident at Ely (Cambridgeshire) where five soldiers had been flogged for protesting about 'a stoppage for their knapsacks'. As an ex-soldier Cobbett was outraged not merely at the poor rations (an example of the kind of corruption that he had protested about himself), but that German troops, mercenaries stationed at Bury St Edmunds, were used to do it.

> *Five hundred lashes* each! Aye, that is right! Flog them; flog them; flog them! They deserve it, and a great deal more. They deserve a flogging at every meal-time. 'Lash them daily, lash them duly'. What, shall the rascals dare to *mutiny*, and that, too, when the German legion is so near at hand! . . . They *deserve* it. O, yes; they merit a double-tailed cat . . . Base rascals! Mutiny for the price of a goat's skin; and, then, upon the appearance of the *German Soldiers*, they take a flogging as quietly as so many trunks of trees! – I do not know what sort of place Ely is; but I really should like to know how the inhabitants looked one another in the face, while this scene was exhibiting in their town. I should like to have been able to see their faces, and hear their observations to one another, at the time. – This occurrence at home will, one would hope, teach *the loyal* a little caution in speaking of the means, which Napoleon employs (or, rather, which they say he employs), in order to get together and discipline his Conscripts. There is scarcely any one of these loyal persons, who has not, at various times, cited the *hand-cuffings*, and other means of *force*, said to be used in drawing out the young men of France; there is scarcely one of the loyal, who has not cited these as means of proof, a complete proof, that the people of France *hate Napoleon and his government*, *assist with reluctance in his wars*, and would *fain see another revolution*. I hope, I say, that the loyal will, hereafter, be more cautious in drawing such conclusions, now that they see, that our 'gallant

defenders' not only require physical restraint, in certain cases, but even a little blood drawn from their backs, and that too, with the aid and assistance of *German* troops.

Political Register, Vol. 15 (1 July 1809), p.993.

It was enough for the government. Cobbett was tried for seditious libel in June 1810, convicted, and spent two years in Newgate Jail. It was not enough to stop him writing however: 'Sir Walter Raleigh wrote his History of the World in a prison; and it was in a prison that Cervantes wrote Don Quixote', he observed in first issue after his imprisonment. There was no break in the regular publication of the *Political Register*.

Yet Cobbett was much more than the maverick journalist he was sometimes described as being. Though he had his eccentricities he had also clear and clearly evolving political principles. Though he was not an open republican and he avoided the kind of anti-religious statements that had so damaged Paine's later reputation, he had a profound respect for Paine's ideas – so much so that in one of the more curious episodes of his life, when Cobbett came back from America after a second period of political exile from 1817–19, he brought with him as a symbolic gesture Tom Paine's bones. While there in 1819, still indefatigably producing his *Political Register* from the other side of the Atlantic, he had given his version of the essential principles of society in words that, while unmistakably his own, were a clear response to Burke's view of society as an inalienable inheritance and would not have disappointed the author of *The Rights of Man*:

Society ought not to exist, if not for the benefit of the whole. It is and must be against the law of nature, if it exists for the benefit of the few and/or the misery of the many. I say, then, distinctly that a society, in which the common labourer, with common health and strength and with economy and sobriety and industry and good morals and good manners, cannot secure a sufficiency of food and raiment, it is a society which

ought not to exist; a society contrary to the law of
nature; a society whose compact is dissolved.

Ibid., Vol. 35, p.115.

William Hone

William Hone (1780–1842) was a radical bookseller, publisher
and the author of numerous pamphlets on political questions
in the early years of the nineteenth century. Born in London
during the Gordon Riots in 1780, he was brought up in a
poor but literate household, learning to read from the Bible
and *Pilgrim's Progress*. His religious doubts began with his
reading Bishop Watson's *Apology for the Bible* (1796). The
event is recorded by him in an autobiographical fragment:

> Bishop Watson's 'Apology for the Bible', in answer
> to Paine's 'Age of Reason' was given to my father,
> and he gave it to me. I only knew the 'Age of Reason'
> existed by his conversing with a friend upon it as a
> mischievous work; its nature I soon understood from
> the Bishop's book. Until the 'Apology' informed me,
> I never conceived the Bible had been, or could be,
> doubted or disbelieved, and, strange to say, although
> I thought Bishop Watson proved the untruth of much
> that Paine had written, yet the Bishop's work alone
> created doubt in me who had never before doubted.
> Cited by Frederick W. Hackwood, p.45.

By the age of 16 he had read Godwin, Holcroft and Owen
and come to the conclusion that 'with the cultivation of the
intellect, Christianity ... would disappear, and Reason
become omnipotent'. Yet his early influences had given a
biblical framework to his thought that was to last the rest of
his life and which was to stand him in good stead when he
was arrested and charged with blasphemy in what was
intended to be a political show-trial. It was for him wholly
natural that in his satires and lampoons of the government
he should turn to literary forms that through the Bible and
the Prayer Book and the Catechism were available to all but

the totally illiterate. In addition to producing a regular newspaper, the *Reformist's Register*, which, like Cobbett's *Weekly Register* with which it was often linked, was reduced to the easily affordable price of twopence in 1817 and dealt with current political topics, Hone also produced individual satires in pamphlet form.

Hone's targets are in keeping with the simple popular style of his satires themselves. Though elsewhere he is capable of appealing to points of principle with as much tenacity as Paine or Wordsworth, his political satire is for the most part directed squarely at the practical details of corruption – sinecures, government pensions, misuse of public funds and, as always, the behaviour of the Prince. *The Poor Man's Litany*, for instance, has an eye for sordid detail to ram home the very simple message that the gap between the rich and the poor is not an accident, but part of the system. Yet on closer inspection the rhyme and the rollicking twelve-syllabic rhythm belong not to the Prayer Book but to a more popular mediaeval tradition where the form of the Litany was adapted and used in secular ballads, a tradition which Hone, a self-educated polymath, knew very well. Thus Pitt and his hated income-tax, invented to pay for the war, take their place beside the other 'ghoulies and ghosties and long-legged beasties/And things that go bump in the night' that the old Cornish Litany was most afraid of.

THE POOR MAN'S LITANY

From four pounds of Bread, at Sixteen-pence price,
And Butter at Eighteen, though not very nice,
And Cheese at a Shilling, though gnaw'd by the mice,
           Good Lord, deliver us!
From stale Clods of Beef, at a Shilling a pound,
Which, in summer, with fly-blows and maggots abound,
Or dried by the wind, and scarce fit for a hound,
           Good Lord, deliver us!
From the Tax upon Income, invented by Pitt,
Though the Great Ones contrive to lose nothing by it,

Yet we who have little are sure to be bit,
           Good Lord, deliver us!
From Taxes Assess'd, now rais'd at a nod,
While Inspectors rule o'er us with their iron rod,
And expect homage paid them like some demi-god,
           Good Lord, deliver us!
From Forestallers, Regraters, and all that curs'd train,
Who, to swell out their bags, will hoard up the grain,
Against which we cry out with our might and main,
           Good Lord, deliver us!
From a Workhouse where hunger and poverty rage,
And distinction's a stranger to birth, sex or age;
Lame and Blind, all must work, or be coop'd in a
    cage,
           Good Lord, deliver us!
From six in a bed in those mansions of woe,
Where nothing but beards, nails, and vermin do grow,
And from picking of Oakum in cellars below,
           Good Lord, deliver us!
From Stickings of Beef, old, wither'd, and tough,
Bread, like Saw-dust and Bran, and of that not enough,
And scarcely a rag to cover our Buff,
           Good Lord, deliver us!
From the tantalized sight of viewing the Great
Luxuriously rolling in coaches of state,
While thousands are starving – for something to eat,
           Good Lord, deliver us!
From feasts and rejoicings, ye Gluttons, abstain,
Since the blessings you boast of but give the Poor
    pain,
And of which one and all so loudly complain,
           Good Lord, deliver us!
But these Burthens remov'd, then united we'll pray,
Both the young and the old, the grave and the gay –
"May the Rulers be happy, and live to be grey;"
Rejoice then, ye Britons, that's our Jubilee day,
          We beseech thee to hear us, Good Lord!

The use of popular satiric poems of this kind was not, of

course, confined to the radicals, though defence of the old abuses became increasingly difficult to sustain once the final defeat of Napoleon at Waterloo and the restoration of the Bourbon monarchy in France meant that the country could no longer be held to be in danger and the charge of treason could no longer be so effectively flung at the reformers. A pamphlet published at this time, for instance, is entitled *Sketches of the Life of Billy Cobb, and the Death of Tommy Pain. To which is Added an Expostulatory Epistle to Mr Hone, the Lunarian.* Though it is anonymous and undated, it is clear that it comes from a pro-Government source and that it was written some time just after Cobbett's return from America with Paine's bones in 1819 and the publication of Hone's *The Man in the Moon* (a Speech from the Throne at the opening of parliament in an imaginary 'lunar' kingdom) published in 1820. What is interesting from our point of view is that it witnesses to the effectiveness of Cobbett's and Hone's criticism of the government by singling out them in turn as its targets. Its tactic is to try and link both with Paine, who had lost much of the popular support he had gained with *The Rights of Man* by his subsequent attacks on religion in *The Age of Reason.* Cobbett's return with Paine's bones was an obvious godsend to such satirists. The pamphlet is presented and illustrated as extracts from a children's chap-book primer of the alphabet. It begins with a reminder of Cobbett's early days in America when he was in the army and his subsequent court-martial:

C WAS A CORPORAL

sent to fight
Against the Yankee-doodles;
To vex and tease, was his delight,
And call his comrades, noodles.

Long time his temper vile they bore,
And suffered him to flout;
But when endurance could no more,
They fairly drummed him out.

His knot they tore, his coat they turned,
    His belts they made him doff;
His loop-ed hat, they took and burned,
    And cut his buttons off.

Then pointed bay'nets at his rear, –
    The "ROGUE'S MARCH" played before;
And Fate decreed he should appear,
    A TURNCOAT evermore.

Having thus branded Cobbett as a traitor at the outset, the
pamphlet then proceeds to Paine:

Old Satan had a darling boy,
    Full equal he to Cain;
Born peace and order to destroy;
    His name was – **THOMAS PAINE**.

Becoming jealous of his son for outdoing him in evil deeds,
Satan decides to kill him, but agrees that his bones shall lie
undisturbed until there passes his grave someone worse than
himself – which happens, of course, when one midnight
Cobbett happens to come along.

The idea is clever enough at the level of a revue-sketch, but
it makes no attempt to meet the attack on poverty and
corruption, begun by Paine and ably continued by Cobbett
and Hone, beyond suggesting that all three are children of a
comic-book Devil. It is a problem always inherent in the use
of nursery-rhyme forms for popular satire. Here, as in Hone's
Litany, the very use of the comic rhymes and metre, effective
and memorable as it can be, to some extent detracts from the
seriousness of the content. Similarly, as in *The Political House
that Jack Built* (see p.160), the effect of Hone's *Litany* is to
belittle the targets of the satire, the oppressors, rather than
to dwell on the grievances of the oppressed. The problem
was solved by turning to another equally well-known form;
the Prayer Book, but only at the expense of creating a further
problem, potentially more dangerous. Thus when Hone
turned to the Ten Commandments, the effect is at once
sharper and more sombre – and it offered his opponents a

way of exploiting virtually the only weapon they could find against him, the charge of blasphemy and irreligion:

> IV. Remember that thou attend the Minister's Levee day; on other days shalt thou speak for him in the House, and fetch and carry, and do all that he commandeth thee to do; but the Levee day is for the glorification of the Minister thy Lord. In it thou shalt do no work in the House, but shall wait upon him, thou, and thy daughter, and thy wife, and the members that are within his influence; for on other days the Minister is inaccessible, but delighteth in the Levee day, wherefore the Minister appointed the Levee day, and chatteth thereon familiarly, and is amused by it.
>
> V. Honour the Regent and the helmets of the Life Guards, that thy stay may be long in the Place, which thy Lord the Minister giveth thee.
>
> VI. Thou shalt not call starving to death a murder.
>
> VII. Thou shalt not call Royal gallivanting adultery.
>
> VIII. Thou shalt not say that to rob the public is to steal.
>
> IX. Thou shalt bear false witness against the People.

Hone's version of the Lord's Prayer is similarly pungent:

> Our Lord, who art in the Treasury, whatsoever be thy name, thy power be prolonged, thy will be done throughout the empire, as it is in each session. Give us our usual sops, and forgive us our occasional absences on divisions; as we promise not to forgive them that divide against thee. Turn us not out of our Places; but keep us in the House of Commons, the Land of Pensions and Plenty; and deliver us from the People. Amen.

His parody of the Catechism combines the usual attack on the Government with one on the monarchy itself, and, because of the explicit nature of the model, it names its targets quite specifically:

Question. WHAT is your name?

Answer. Lick Spittle.

Q. Who gave you this name?

A. My Sureties to the Ministry, in my Political Change, wherein I was made a Member of the Majority, the Child of Corruption, and a Locust to devour the good Things of this Kingdom.

Q. What did your Sureties then for you?

A. They did promise and vow three things in my Name. First, that I should renounce the Reformists and all their Words, the pomps and vanity of Popular Favour, and all the sinful lusts of Independence. Secondly, that I should believe all the Articles of the Court Faith. And thirdly, that I should keep the Minister's sole Will and Commandments, and walk in the same, all the days of my life.

Q. Dost thou not think that thou art bound to believe and to do as they have promised for thee?

A. Yes, verily, and for my own sake, so I will; and I heartily thank our heaven-born Ministry, that they have called me to this state of elevation, through my own flattery, cringing, and bribery; and I shall pray to their successors to give me their assistance, that I may continue the same unto my life's end.

Q. Rehearse the Articles of thy Belief.

A. I believe in GEORGE, the Regent Almighty, Maker of New Streets, and Knights of the Bath.

And in the present Ministry, his only choice, who were conceived of Toryism, brought forth of WILLIAM PITT, suffered loss of Place under CHARLES JAMES FOX, were execrated, dead and buried. In a few months they rose again from their minority; they re-ascended to the Treasury benches, and sit at the right hand of a little man with a large wig; from whence they laugh at the Petitions of the People who may pray for Reform, and that the sweat of their brow may procure them Bread.

Yet, of course, the effectiveness of these parodies lies not just in their use of popular literary forms. The Ten Commandments, the Lord's Prayer, and the Catechism were well-known because they were part of the liturgy of a state religion whose founder had been conspicuously poor, humble and chaste. It was hard for the person in the pew in 1817 to see any of these characteristics in the habits of the ruling-class that believed so strongly in the virtues of religion for the masses. To use such liturgical models for this kind of satire was more effective than any use of secular literature would have been – and (though it was in the interests of neither side to admit it) it was precisely because of this implicit moral comment, inherent in these forms, rather than in the more comic litanies or the nursery-rhymes, that Hone was singled out for prosecution for blasphemy. Hone, however, in spite of the propaganda assiduously put out against him, was no Tom Paine. Whatever his religious doubts at this period (he later was reconverted and became a Baptist), he had been deeply moved by his early reading of Bunyan and he met the charges against him with all the moral fervour of Christian meeting the fiend Apollyon in *Pilgrim's Progress*.

From the government's point of view Hone's three trials in December 1817 were a political and public relations disaster. The jury had been carefully chosen (or rigged) with a view to gaining a conviction and Hone himself had actually been denied access to the charges against him so that he would be unable to prepare his defence. Though the offending pamphlets had been withdrawn from circulation in May, after his first arrest, the trial, as is the way of such things, called fresh attention to them and the reading of them aloud in Court provoked widespread laughter. Hone conducted his own defence, citing a long tradition of biblical parodies for political purposes beginning with Luther (who had himself parodied the Lord's Prayer) and ending with the current Dean of Canterbury and George Canning, a member of the government. On the subject of the Creeds he was even able to quote the father of the presiding judge, Lord Ellenborough, who had been Bishop of Carlisle, in support of his case. By an interesting quirk of fate Lord Ellenborough's family name was Law. He had an ominous reputation from his conduct of previous political trials for denying prisoners their legal rights and for giving openly biased directions to the jury. It was he who had secured Cobbett's imprisonment in 1810 for protesting against the savage flogging of the militia men at Ely. But this was to be his last trial. As a consequence of his failure to secure a conviction, for which he had as usual shamelessly tried to bias the jury, he resigned and within a few months was dead.

On his acquittal of all three charges of blasphemy Hone became a popular hero. He was carried shoulder-high through the streets of London, and a public subscription, to which many of the clergy donated, was opened to pay his expenses. The anonymous pamphleteer of *The Life of Billy Cobb* could do no more than make the pun on Hone's name (a 'hone' is another word for a whetstone) and suggest that it went to pay bribes to the jury:

> This is a HONE, by subscription 'twas oiled,
> Because it the measures of Justice had foiled.

Almost as much at a loss for an argument as a rhyme, he concludes bitterly:

> Celebrity you clearly gained
>   At Guildhall – I suppose a
> 'ssistance was previously obtained
>   From Barristers, – sub rosa.
>
> On that, of course, you built defence,
>   Success has made you daring;
> And now your stock of impudence,
>   Is almost beyond bearing.

Hone's acquittal was the climax of a series of successful defences by radicals against government prosecution. In June 1817 Dr James Watson, who had attempted to organise an actual revolution beginning with a riot at Spa Fields in North London – an event potentially much more dangerous to the state than Peterloo, had been acquitted when it was discovered that the principal witness for the prosecution, John Castle, was a paid government informer who had helped to start the violence. His son, popularly known as 'Young Watson', had recited Southey's *Wat Tyler* while leading an abortive attack on the Tower of London. Later in the same month T.J. Wooler, editor of another radical periodical, *The Black Dwarf*, was acquitted of two charges of seditious libel. Cobbett was exultant: it was the beginning of the end at least of legal coercion and repression. 'Mr Hone's Trial', he wrote, 'and his meritorious conduct will be . . . ranked along with those of William Penn . . . and the rest of the brave men who have resisted tyranny's favourite weapon'. Reform was still more than a decade away, but the climate of public opinion was slowly changing.

4 The Architecture of the State

The Metaphor

Among the most persistent political metaphors of the period is that of the state as a work of architecture. For a country like England the image had a special appropriateness, as those who used it quickly realised. Unlike France, England had always been an architecturally conservative country, not merely in the sense that new fashions spread more slowly and were often modified by vernacular and traditional ways of working as they were absorbed, but also in the reluctance of the landowners who were modernising their country houses to pull down the existing buildings and start afresh. Whereas the glory of the great French chateaux of the seventeenth and eighteenth centuries was their architectural homogeneity, the distinctive quality of the English great houses was a historical variety that revealed the age and ancestry of the house – and, of course, by extension, the house-owner. Thus country houses like Penshurst or Knole, as well as even the main royal residence, Hampton Court, still retained their mediaeval great halls alongside the sixteenth, seventeenth and eighteenth-century additions. Then, as now, English people grew up surrounded by a visible sense of their own past, enshrined in their buildings.

Architectural metaphors therefore were at one level simple enough for even the least educated to understand, while having an equal appeal to those capable of appreciating the history they represented. On the one hand, they offered in a visible and concrete form the high abstract idea of the state as a human artifact, while at the same time drawing on associations with the parallel sequence of organic imagery by suggesting that great buildings were things that had grown 'naturally' over many centuries and represented more than the rational planning of any one architect. Conversely, the undeniable fact that many of the great buildings of England were dilapidated and in a poor state of repair was seized upon by those who were more impressed by the corruption of the state than by its vaunted antiquity.

As one might expect, the image makes a frequent appearance in Burke:

> The science of constructing a commonwealth, or renovating it, or reforming it, is, like every other science, not to be taught a priori. . . . it is with infinite caution that any man ought to venture upon pulling down an edifice which has answered in any tolerable degree for ages the common purposes of society, or on building it up again, without having models and patterns of approved utility before his eyes.
>
> *Reflections*, p.90.

Later, discussing the new local government structure of France, he combines the architectural metaphor with the organic by means of reference to landscape gardening – not unmindful, one suspects, of a long tradition of such metaphors in Shakespeare: *Richard II*, for example, or the specific application of the image to France in Burgundy's speech in *Henry V*. The allusion to Shakespeare is combined with a reference to the well-known difference between the regular geometry of the traditional style of French landscape gardening exemplified by someone like Le Notre, and the studied irregularity of the English style of 'Capability' Brown, Humphrey Repton or Richard Payne Knight, which conformed more to 'nature', and which had recently become fashionable all over Europe, including France itself. Thus the present revolutionary reformers, writes Burke, 'are in no way embarrassed with an endeavour to accommodate the new building to an old one, either in the walls or on the foundations. . . . The French builders, clearing away as mere rubble whatever they found, . . . like their ornamental gardeners, form . . . everything into an exact level. . . .' (*Reflections*, pp.255–56).

Other conservative writers were quick to exploit Burke's imagery. Hannah More, for instance, in *Village Politics*, part of which was quoted earlier (p.96) makes skilful use of it as a symbol of stability and order.

> *Jack.* I'll tell thee a story. When Sir John married, my Lady, who is a little fantastical, and likes to do everything like the French, begged him to pull down yonder fine old castle, and build it up in her frippery way. No, says Sir John; what shall I pull down this noble building, raised by the wisdom of my brave ancestors; which outstood the civil wars, and only underwent a little needful repair at the Revolution; and which all my neighbours come to take a pattern by – shall I pull it all down, I say, only because there may be a dark closet or an inconvenient room or two in it? My lady mumpt and grumbled; but the castle was let stand, and a glorious building it is, though there may be a trifling fault or two, and tho' a few decays may want stopping; so now and then they mend a little thing, and they'll go on mending, I dare say, as they have leisure, to the end of the chapter, if they are let alone. But no pull-me-down works.
>
> *Village Politics*, pp.8–9.

The Political House that Jack Built

William Hone had achieved notoriety in 1819 by combining Burke's architectural metaphor with the form of a nursery-rhyme in *The Political House that Jack Built*. In the Dedication to 'Dr Slop' (a reference to a character in Sterne's *Tristram Shandy*) the readers of this 'juvenile publication' are described as 'the nursery of children six feet high'. Hone's illustrator, who was soon to become a personal friend, was a talented young cartoonist called George Cruikshank.

The motto for *The Political House* was taken from William Cowper's well-known poem, *The Task*, which among other things paints a picture of peaceful and civilised rural life isolated from the wars, worldliness and corruption of the outside world. It is typical of the many levels of Hone's satire that subtle but pointed literary references of this kind should find their way into something apparently fashioned in the shape of children's verse. The passage chosen offers a clear forerunner to Burke's own architectural metaphor:

> ------Many, whose sequester'd lot
> Forbids their interference, looking on,
> Anticipate perforce some dire event;
> And, seeing the old castle of the state,
> That promis'd once more firmness, so assail'd,
> That all its tempest-beaten turrets shake,
> Stand motionless expectants of its fall.

Each repeat of the cumulative structure of the rhyme is illustrated by a Cruikshank engraving to provide an ironic commentary on the words which, if read by themselves, would be entirely harmless; perhaps a sign of caution from Hone's trial of less than two years before, but in any case a brilliant rhetorical device. It begins:

THIS IS
THE WEALTH
that lay
In the House that Jack Built

The 'wealth' in the illustration, however, turns out not to be money but nothing less than the ancient liberties of the English people: Magna Carta, Habeas Corpus and, no less significantly, in view of the attack on the Church to follow, a book that looks suspiciously like the Bible – in short, the same priceless 'possessions' that Burke had described by a similar fiscal metaphor as constituting a legacy handed down from past generations. The next repeat runs:

THESE ARE
THE VERMIN
That plunder the Wealth,
That lay in the House
That Jack Built.

The illustration shows not rats, but the professions: the law, the church, the army, etc. The following repeat shows a printing-press:

THIS IS
THE THING
that in spite of new Acts,
And attempts to restrain it,
by Soldiers or Tax,
Will *poison* the Vermin,
That plunder the Wealth,
That lay in the House,
That Jack built.

The 'Vermin' are mercilessly detailed in the succeeding repeats until we reach the Prince Regent himself:

This is **THE MAN** – all shaven and shorn,
All cover'd with Orders – and all forlorn:
THE DANDY OF SIXTY
who bows with a grace,
And has *taste* in wigs, collars,
cuirasses and lace;
Who, to tricksters and fools,
leaves the State and its treasure,
And, when Britain's in tears,
sails about at his pleasure:
Who spurn'd from his presence
the Friends of his youth,
And now has not one
who will tell him the truth.

The charge is not that he is corrupt or foolish, but that he is in the end to be pitied for having no friends, must make this in its own way one of the most devastating lampoons ever written – even of that favourite target, the Prince Regent. Moreover, the repetitive and cumulative structure of the nursery-rhyme meant that these lines were to be repeated over and over again as the other bizarre contents and associates of the 'house' (also, of course, in political circles the abbreviation for either the House of Commons or House of Lords) were duly paraded for inspection.

Hone's *Political House* was an enormous success. It went through 54 editions and inspired a host of imitations and loyalist replies: *A Parody on the Political House that Jack Built: or the Real House that Jack Built* by M. Adams (1820) – printed, interestingly, by none other than Joseph Johnson; *The Real Constitutional House that Jack Built* (1820); and *The Loyalists House that Jack Built* among others. The frontispieces tell their own story.

Thomas Love Peacock

It was against this background of parody and counter-parody that Thomas Love Peacock (1785–1866) began work on his satirical romance of ancient Wales, *The Misfortunes of Elphin*. Though by no means a radical, Peacock was a close friend of Shelley and committed to the idea of constitutional reform. He also had a keen eye for the absurdities of the political debates of his day. *The Misfortunes of Elphin* was not published until 1829, but its origins lie a decade earlier when he had just married his Welsh-speaking wife and started research into Welsh history and folklore. The architectural metaphor as a vehicle of political satire was therefore in his mind right from the start.

In this story of the sixth century A.D., Wales is a semi-mythical kingdom, as rich in treasure as in bards. The greatest source of its prosperity is the fertile low-lying plain to the west of the Cambrian Mountains and now wholly covered by the waters of Cardigan Bay. Even in the sixth century, Peacock tells us, much of this land was actually below sea-level, but the water was kept out by an enormous sea-wall running from north to south across the entrance to the bay:

> Watchtowers were erected along the embankment, and watchmen were appointed to guard against the first approaches of damage or decay. The whole of these towers, and their companies of guards, were subordinate to a central castle, which commanded the sea-

port already mentioned, and wherein dwelt Prince Seithenyn ap Seithyn Saidi, who held the office of Arglwyd Gorwarchiedwad yr Argae Breninawl, which signifies, in English, Lord High Commissioner of Royal Embankment; and he executed it as a personage so denominated might be expected to do: he drank the profits, and left the embankment to his deputies, who left it to their assistants, who left it to itself.

> *The Misfortunes of Elphin, The Novels of Thomas Love Peacock*, ed. David Garnett (1948), p.555.

Prince Elphin is sent to remonstrate with Seithenyn on the state of the embankment. The latter, as usual, is drinking with his friends. His argument for reverencing the wall on account of its age and the fact that it was created by their ancestors is, of course, a direct reference to Burke:

> "Prince Seithenyn," said Elphin, "I have visited you on a subject of deep moment. Reports have been brought to me, that the embankment, which has been so long intrusted to your care, is in a state of dangerous decay."
>
> "Decay," said Seithenyn, "is one thing, and danger is another. Every thing that is old must decay. That the embankment is old, I am free to confess; that it is somewhat rotten in parts, I will not altogether deny; that it is any the worse for that, I do most sturdily gainsay. It does its business well: it works well: it keeps out water from the land, and it lets in the wine upon the High Commission of Embankment. Cupbearer, fill. Our ancestors were wiser than we: they built it in their wisdom; and, if we should be so rash as to try to mend it, we should only mar it."
>
> "The stonework," said Teithrin, "is sapped and mined: the piles are rotten, broken, and dislocated: the floodgates and sluices are leaky and creaky."
>
> "That is the beauty of it," said Seithenyn. "Some parts of it are rotten, and some parts of it are sound."

"It is well," said Elphin, "that some parts are sound: it were better that all were so."

"So I have heard some people say before," said Seithenyn; "perverse people, blind to venerable antiquity: that very unamiable sort of people, who are in the habit of indulging their reason. But I say, the parts that are rotten give elasticity to those that are sound: they give them elasticity, elasticity, elasticity. If it were all sound, it would break by its own obstinate stiffness: the soundness is checked by the rottenness, and the stiffness is balanced by the elasticity. There is nothing so dangerous as innovation. See the waves in the equinoctial storms, dashing and clashing, roaring and pouring, spattering and battering, rattling and battling against it. I would not be so presumptuous as to say, I could build any thing that would stand against them half an hour; and here this immortal old work, which God forbid the finger of modern mason should bring into jeopardy, this immortal work has stood for centuries, and will stand for centuries more, if we let it alone. It is well: it works well: let well alone. Cupbearer, fill. It was half rotten when I was born, and that is a conclusive reason why it should be three parts rotten when I die."

At this point Peacock has very cleverly introduced a new element into the argument. Though the architecture of the eighteenth century was often magnificent, its record of building *maintenance* was strikingly poor. Hallowed ancient buildings (such as Lichfield Cathedral) were found to be in ruinous state and on the verge of collapse. Though Burke compares the state to a building, he nowhere suggests that it might need repair or restoration or adaptation to meet altered climatic conditions. Buildings are in the end functional: they exist to perform a service – or they have no value:

> "And after all," said Seithenyn, "the worst that could happen would be the overflow of a spring tide, for that was the worst that happened before the

embankment was thought of; and, if the high water, should come in, as it did before, the low water would go out again, as it did before. We should be no deeper in it than our ancestors were, and we could mend as easily as they could make."

"The level of the sea," said Teithrin, "is materially altered."

"The level of the sea!" exclaimed Seithenyn. "Who ever heard of such a thing as altering the level of the sea? Alter the level of that bowl of wine before you, in which, as I sit here, I see a very ugly reflection of your very goodlooking face. Alter the level of that: drink up the reflection: let me see the face without the reflection, and leave the sea to level itself."

Ibid., pp.560–62.

Shortly afterwards a combination of high winds and spring tides breaches the wall, and the sea pours through. Prince Seithenyn, insisting to the end that the cause must be a conspiracy of enemies rather than the rising of the sea, attempts to hold back the flood by brandishing his sword and drunkenly shouting defiance. In the ensuing inundation the greater part of Wales is flooded and the remnant of the dispirited survivors have to flee into the mountains that are all that is left of the once-prosperous kingdom – where they remain to this day.

Thomas Carlyle: The Fall of the Bastille

If, in Peacock's fable, it is the elemental forces of nature that finally overwhelm the bastions of the constitution, for Carlyle, who published his *French Revolution* in 1837 after a second French Revolution in 1830 when, yet again, the fate of a government and a constitution was decided by the Paris mob, those natural forces have become merged with the irresistible tides of human history. In Carlyle we see it is the Paris mob itself that becomes the raging waters or the fire that will destroy the Bastille, here, in this final extract, a symbol of the confusion and corruption of the *ancien régime*:

To describe this Seige of the Bastille (thought to be one of the most important in History) perhaps transcends the talent of mortals. Could one but, after infinite reading, get to understand so much as the plan of the building! But there is open Esplanade, at the end of the Rue Saint-Antoine; there are such Forecourts, *Cour Avance, Cour de l'Orme*, arched Gateway (where Louis Tournay now fights); then new drawbridges, dormant-bridges, rampart-bastions, and the grim Eight Towers; a labyrinthic Mass, high-frowning there, of all ages from twenty years to four hundred and twenty; – beleaguered, in this its last hour, as we said, by mere Chaos come again! Ordnance of all calibres, throats of all capacities; men of all plans, every man his own engineer: seldom since the war of Pygmies and Cranes was there seen so anomalous a thing. Half-pay Elie is home for a suit of regimentals; no one would heed him in coloured clothes: half-pay Hulin is haranguing Guardes Françaises in the Place de Grève. Frantic Patriots pick up the grapeshots; bear them, still hot (or seemingly so), to the Hôtel-de-Ville: – Paris, you perceive, is to be burnt! Flesselles is 'pale to the very lips,' for the roar of the multitude grows deep. Paris wholly has got to the acme of its frenzy; whirled, all ways, by panic madness. At every street-barricade, there whirls simmering a minor whirlpool, – strengthening the barricade, since God knows what is coming; and all minor whirlpools play distractedly into that Grand Fire-Mahlstrom which is lashing round the Bastille.

And so it lashes and it roars. Cholat the wine-merchant has become an impromptu cannoneer. See Georget, of the Marine Service, fresh from Brest, ply the King of Siam's cannon. Singular (if we were not used to the like): Georget lay, last night, taking his ease at his inn; the King of Siam's cannon also lay, knowing nothing of *him*, for a hundred years. Yet now, at the right instant, they have got together, and discourse eloquent music. For, hearing what was toward, Georget sprang from the Brest Diligence, and

ran. Gardes Françaises also will be here, with real
artillery: were not the walls so thick! – Upwards from
the Esplanade, horizontally from all neighbouring
roofs and windows, flashes one irregular deluge of
musketry, without effect. The Invalides lie flat, firing
comparatively at their ease from behind stone; hardly
through portholes, show the tip of a nose. We fall,
shot; and make no impression!

Let conflagration rage; of whatsoever is combustible!
Guard-rooms are burnt, Invalides mess-rooms. A
distracted 'Perukemaker with two fiery torches' is for
burning 'the saltpetres of the Arsenal'; – had not a
woman run screaming; had not a Patriot, with some
tincture of Natural Philosophy, instantly struck the
wind out of him (butt of musket on pit of stomach),
overturned barrels, and stayed the devouring element.
A young beautiful lady, seized escaping in these
Outer Courts, and thought falsely to be De Launay's
daughter, shall be burnt in De Launay's sight; she lies
swooned on a paillasse: but again a Patriot, it is brave
Aubin Bonnemere the old soldier, dashes in, and
rescues her. Straw is burnt; three cartloads of it, hauled
thither, go up in white smoke: almost to the choking
of Patriotism itself; so that Elie had, with singed
brows, to drag back one cart; and Reole the 'gigantic
haberdasher' another. Smoke as of Tophet; confusion
as of Babel; noise as of the Crack of Doom!

Blood flows; the aliment of new madness. The
wounded are carried into houses of the Rue Cerisaie;
the dying leave their last mandate not to yield till the
accursed Stronghold fall. And yet, alas, how fall? The
walls are so thick! Deputations, three in number, arrive
from the Hôtel-de-Ville; Abbé Fauchet (who was of
one) can say, with what almost superhuman courage
of benevolence. These wave their Town-flag in the
arched Gateway; and stand, rolling their drum; but to
no purpose. In such Crack of Doom, De Launay
cannot hear them, dare not believe them: they return,
with justified rage, the whew of lead still singing in
their ears. What to do? The Fire-Invalides cannon, to

wet the touchholes; they unfortunately cannot squirt so high; but produce only clouds of spray. Individuals of classical knowledge propose *catapults*. Santerre, the sonorous Brewer of the Suburb Saint-Antoine, advises rather that the place be fired, by a 'mixture of phosorous and oil-of-turpentine spouted up through forcing pumps': O Spinola-Santerre, hast thou the mixture *ready*? Every man his own engineer! And still the firedeluge abates not: even women are firing, and Turks; at least one woman (with her sweetheart), and one Turk. Gardes Françaises have come: real cannon, real cannoneers. Usher Maillard is busy; half-pay Elie, half-pay Hulin rage in the midst of thousands.

How the great Bastille Clock ticks (inaudible) in its Inner Court there, at its ease, hour after hour; as if nothing special, for it or the world, were passing! It tolled One when the firing began; and is now pointing towards Five, and still the firing slakes not. – Far down, in their vaults, the seven Prisoners hear muffled din as of earthquakes; their Turnkeys answer vaguely.

Wo to thee, De Launay, with thy poor hundred Invalides! Broglie is distant, and his ears heavy: Besenval hears, but can send no help. One poor troop of Hussars has crept, reconnoitering, cautiously along the Quais, as far as the Pont Neuf. "We are come to join you," said the Captain; for the crowd seems shoreless. A large-headed dwarfish individual, of smoke-bleared aspect, shambles forward, opening his blue lips, for there is sense in him; and croaks: "Alight then, and give up your arms!" The Hussar-Captain is too happy to be escorted to the Barriers, and dismissed on Parole. Who the squat individual was? Men answer, it is M. Marat, author of the excellent pacific *Avis au Peuple*! Great truly, O thou remarkable Dog-leech, is this thy day of emergence and new-birth: and yet this same day come four years – ! – But let the curtains of the Future hang.

What shall De Launay do? One thing only De Launay could have done: what he said he would do. Fancy him sitting, from the first, with lighted taper, within arm's length of the Powder-Magazine; motion-less, like old Roman Senator, or Bronze Lampholder; coldly apprising Thuriot, and all men, by a slight motion of his eye, what his resolution was: – Harmless he sat there, while unharmed; but the King's Fortress, meanwhile, could, might, would, or should, in nowise be surrendered, save to the King's Messenger: one old man's life is worthless, so it be lost with honour; but think, ye brawling *canaille*, how will it be when a whole Bastille springs skyward! – In such statuesque, taper-holding attitude, one fancies De Launay might have left Thuriot, the red Clerks of the Basoche, Curé of Saint-Stephen and all the tag-rag-and-bobtail of the world, to work their will. . . .

Great is the combined voice of men; the utterance of their *instincts*, which are truer than their *thoughts*: it is the greatest a man encounters, among the sounds and shadows which make up this World of Time. He who can resist that, has his footing somewhere *beyond* Time. De Launay could not do it. Distracted, he hovers between two; hopes in the middle of despair; surrenders not his Fortress; declares that he will blow it up, seizes torches to blow it up, and does not blow it. Unhappy old De Launay, it is the death-agony of thy Bastille and thee! Jail, Jailoring and Jailor, all three, such as they may have been, must finish.

For four hours now has the World-Bedlam roared: call it the World-Chimaera, blowing fire! The poor Invalides have sunk under their battlements, or rise only with reversed muskets: they have made a white flag of napkins; go beating the *chamade*, or seeming to beat, for one can hear nothing. The very Swiss at the Portcullis look weary of firing; disheartened in the fire-deluge: a porthole at the drawbridge is opened, as by one that would speak. See Juisser Maillard, the shifty man! On his plank, swinging over the abyss of that stone Ditch; plank resting on parapet, balanced by weight of Patriots, – he hovers perilous: such a Dove towards such an Ark! Deftly, thou shifty Usher: one man already fell; and lies smashed, far down there, against the masonry! Usher Maillard falls not: deftly, unerring he walks, with outspread palm. The Swiss holds a paper through his port-hole; the shifty Usher snatches it, and returns. Terms of surrender: Pardon, immunity to all! Are they accepted? – "*Foi d'officier, On the word of an officer,*" answers half-pay Hulin, – or half-pay Elie, for men do not agree on it, "they are!" Sinks the drawbridge, – Usher Maillard bolting it when down; rushes-in the living deluge: the Bastille is fallen! *Victoire! la Bastille est prise!*

The French Revolution, Vol. I, pp.189–94.

Chronological Table

Date	Contemporary events in England	in France	Publications
1756	Godwin b.		
1757	Blake b.		Burke, *Enquiry into the Sublime and the Beautiful*
1759	Burns b.		James Woodforde begins Diary
1762	George IV b.		
1763	Cobbett b.		
1770	Wordsworth b.		Rousseau, *Confessions*
1772	Coleridge b.		
1774	Paine goes to America Southey b.	Louis XV d. Accession of Louis XVI	
1776	American independence		Paine, *Common Sense*
1778			Fanny Burney, *Evelina*
1780	Gordon Riots Hone b.		
1783	Pitt becomes Prime Minister		Blair, *Lectures on Rhetoric and Belles Lettres*
1784	Charlotte Smith follows her husband to France		
1785	Cobbett goes to Canada		David, *The Oath of the Horatii*
1786	Fanny Burney accepts Court appointment		
1787	Paine returns to England	Charlotte Smith leaves her husband	Gregory's translation of Lowth's *Sacred Poetry of the Hebrews*

Date	*Contemporary events*		*Publications*
	in England	*in France*	
1788			Blake, *All Religions are One*
1789		National Assembly convened Tennis Court Oath Fall of the Bastille	Blake, *Songs of Innocence* Price, *Discourse on the Love of Our Country* David, *Lictors returning to Brutus the Bodies of his Sons*
1790			Blake, *The French Revolution* Burke, *Reflections on the Revolution in France*
1791	Price d. Wordsworth goes to France 'King and Country' riots in Birmingham; Priestley's house and library burned Cobbett returns to England	Lous XIV and Marie Antoinette try to escape and are brought back from Varennes	Paine, *The Rights of Man*, Part I
1792	Reeves founds The Association Paine flees to France Shelley b. Cobbett flees to France and then America Southey expelled from Westminster School Cruikshank b.	Wordsworth meets Annette Vallon Paine member of Assembly September Massacres Wordsworth's daughter b. France invades Savoy and Holland Republic declared	Paine, *Rights of Man*, Part II Charlotte Smith, *Desmond* Wollstonecraft, *Rights of Women*
1793	War with France Fanny Burney marries M. d'Arblay	Execution of Louis XVI and Marie Antoinette Reign of Terror Paine arrested	Eaton, *Politics for the People* begins publication Godwin, *Political Justice* More, *Village Politics* Paine, *Age of Reason*, Part I

Date	Contemporary events in England	in France	Publications
1793 cont.		Mary Wollstonecraft meets Imlay in Paris	Wordsworth, *Letter to the Bishop of Llandaff*
1794	Southey and Coleridge meet and plan Pantisocracy Priestley emigrates to America	Fall of Robespierre Paine released	Blake, *Songs of Experience* Burns, "Is there for Honest Poverty" Coleridge and Southey, *The Fall of Robespierre* Paine, *Age of Reason*, Part II
1795	Riot against King New Treason Act	Napoleon quells insurrection of Vendemiaire	Coleridge, *Conciones ad Populum* Coleridge, *Moral & Political Lecture* More, *Cheap Repository Tracts* begin publication *Politics for the People* closes
1796	Eaton escapes to America Burns d.	Beaupuy killed	Coleridge, *The Watchman* Watson, *Apology for the Bible* Wordsworth, *The Borderers*
1797	Burke d. Marriage of Godwin and Mary Wollstonecraft who dies in childbirth		
1798	William and Dorothy Wordsworth and Coleridge go to Germany Irish Rebellion	Napoleon goes to Egypt Nelson destroys French fleet at Battle of the Nile	Southey, 'The Battle of Blenheim' Wordsworth and Coleridge, *Lyrical Ballads*
1799			
1800	Cobbett returns to England		*Lyrical Ballads*, 2nd edn.
1801	Pitt resigns Addington Prime Minister		

Date	Contemporary events in England	in France	Publications
1802	Fanny Burney goes to France and is trapped there until 1812 by renewal of war James Woodforde d.	Paine goes to America Peace of Amiens Wordsworth revisits Annette at Calais	*Cobbett's Political Register* *Lyrical Ballads*, 3rd edn. Wordsworth, *Milton! Thou shouldst be living this hour*
1803	Eaton returns from America and is jailed for 15 months		
1804	Blake tried for treason Pitt Prime Minster	Napoleon crowned Emperor	
1805	Battle of Trafalgar Nelson d.		Wordsworth, first draft of *The Prelude* completed
1806	Pitt d. Charlotte Smith d.		
1807		France invades Portugal	
1808		Spanish king deposed Joseph Bonaparte installed on Spanish throne British expedition in Portugal	
1809	Paine d. (in America)		Wordsworth, *The Convention of Cintra*
1810	Shelley sent down from Oxford Cobbett sentenced to 2 years gaol		Shelley, *The Necessity of Atheism*
1811	Shelley elopes with Harriet Westbrook		

Date	Contemporary events in England	in France	Publications
1811 cont.	George declared Prince Regent		
1812	Shelley goes to Ireland Liverpool Prime Minister Eaton prosecuted	Napoleon invades Russia	Shelley, *A Letter to Lord Ellenborough*
1813	Eaton prosecuted		Shelley, *Queen Mab*
1814	Eaton d. Shelley elopes with Mary Godwin	Napoleon exiled in Elba	
1815		Battle of Waterloo	
1816	Suicide of Harriet Shelley Spa Fields Riot, London		
1817	Suspension of Habeas Corpus Cobbett flees to America Trials of Hone		Hone's liturgical parodies *Hone's Weekly Commentary* *Three Trials of William Hone* Shelley, 'Ozymandias'
1818	Shelleys go to Italy		Hone, *Political House that Jack Built* Mary Shelley, *Frankenstein*
1819	Peterloo Cobbett returns from America with Paine's bones The Six Acts		Shelley, 'The Masque of Anarchy'; 'England in 1819'; 'Song to the Men of England'
1820	George III d. Accession of George IV Trial of Queen Caroline		Hone, *The Man in the Moon* *Life of Billy Cobb and the Death of Tommy Pain* *Real Constitutional House that Jack Built*

Bibliography

(Place of publication is London unless stated otherwise.)

Primary Sources

Adams, M., *A Parody on the Constitutional House that Jack Built, or the Real House that Jack Built*, second edition (published by C. Chapple, Pall-Mall, 1820).

Anonymous, *The Loyalist's House that Jack Built: The British Constitution Triumphant; or A Picture of a Radical Conclave* (printed by Dean and Munday, Threadneedle St. for S. Knights, Sweetings-Alley, Royal Exchange, n.d.).

——, *The Loyal Man in the Moon*, by the author of *The Constitutional House that Jack Built*, third edition (printed for C. Chapple, Pall-Mall).

——, *The Real Constitutional House that Jack Built*, thirteenth edition (printed for J. Asperne, Cornhill, 1820).

——, *Sketches of the Life of Billy Cobb and the Death of Tommy Pain, to which is added An Expostulatory Epistle to Mr. Hone, the Lunarian*, by the author of the Dorchester Guide, second edition (printed and sold by Dean and Munday, Threadneedle St. and J. Chappel & Son, Royal Exchange, n.d.).

Blair, Hugh, *Lectures on Rhetoric and Belles Lettres* (1783).

Burke, Edmund, *Reflections on the Revolution in France*, seventh edition (1790).

Burney, Fanny, *Diary & Letters of Madame d'Arblay*, ed. Charlotte Barrett, 6 vols (1905).

——, *The Journals and Letters of Fanny Burney, (Madame d'Arblay)*, (Oxford), Vol. I, ed. Joyce Hemlow et. al. (1972); Vol. III, ed. Joyce Hemlow et al. (1973); Vol. V, ed. Joyce Hemlow et. al. (1975); Vol. VI, ed. Joyce Hemlow et. al. (1975); Vol. VIII, ed. Peter Hughes et. al. (1980).

Carlyle, Thomas, *The French Revolution*, 2 vols (1900).

Coleridge, Samuel Taylor, *Aids to Reflection*, second edition (1831).

——, *Collected Letters*, ed. E.L. Griggs, 6 vols (Oxford, 1957–61).

——, *Lectures 1795 On Politics and Religion*, ed. Lewis Patton and Peter Mann – *Collected Works of S.T. Coleridge*, Vol. I (1971).

Coleridge, *The Watchman*, ed. Lewis Patton *Collected Works*, Vol. 2 (1970).

Eaton, Daniel Isaac, *Politics for the People: or a Salmagundy for Swine*, Radical Periodicals of Great Britain (New York, 1968).

Gillray, James, *The Satirical Etchings of James Gillray*, ed. Draper Hill (New York, 1976).

Godwin, William, *Enquiry Concerning Political Justice, and its Influence on Morals and Happiness*, facsimile of third edition (1797) with variant readings from first and second editions, 3 vols, ed. F.E.L. Priestley (Toronto, 1946).

Hartley, David, *Observations on Man, his Frame, his Duties, and his Expectations*, 2 vols (1749).

Hone, William, *The Man in the Moon*, ninth edition (1820).

——, *The Political House that Jack Built*, third edition (1819).

——, *The Three Trials of William Hone* (1817).

Lowth, Robert, *Lectures on the Sacred Poetry of the Hebrews*, trs. G. Gregory (1784).

More, Hannah, *Village Politics. Addressed to all the Mechanics, Journeymen, and Day Labourers, in Great Britain*, by Will Chip, a country carpenter (Canterbury, 1793).

Paine, Thomas, *Rights of Man, Writings of Thomas Paine*, ed. Moncure Daniel Conway (A.M.S. Press, New York, 1967), Vol. II.

Peacock, Thomas Love, *The Novels of Thomas Love Peacock*, ed. David Garnett (1948).

Price, Richard, *A Discourse on the Love of our Country* (1789).

Priestley, Joseph, *Letters to the Right Hon. Edmund Burke, Occasioned by his Reflections on the Revolution in France* (Birmingham, 1791).

Rickwood, Edgell (ed.), *Radical Squibs & Loyalist Ripostes: Satirical Pamphlets of the Regency Period, 1819–1821*, illustrated by George Cruikshank and others (Bath, 1971).

Shelley, Percy Bysshe, *Selected Poetry and Prose*, ed. K.N. Cameron (New York, 1951).

Smith, Charlotte, *Desmond. A Novel*, reprinted (New York, 1974).

Wollstonecraft, Mary, *A Vindication of the Rights of Men, in a Letter to the Right Hon. Edmund Burke; occasioned by his Reflections on the Revolution in France* (1790).

——, *A Vindication of the Rights of Women, with Strictures on Political and Moral Subjects* (1792).

Woodforde, James, *A Country Parson: James Woodforde's Diary 1759–1802*, Introduction by Ronald Blythe (Oxford, 1985).

Wordsworth, William, *The Prelude*, 1805 text, eds Jonathan

Wordsworth, M.H. Abrams and Stephen Gill (Norton Critical edition, New York, 1979).
——, *The Prose Works of William Wordsworth*, eds W.J.B. Owen and Jane Worthington Smyser, Vol. 1 (Oxford, 1974).

Secondary Sources

Aarsleff, Hans, *From Locke to Saussure: Essays on the Study of Language and Intellectual History* (Minneapolis, 1982).
Altick, R.D., *The English Common Reader: A Social History of the Mass Reading Public, 1800–1900* (Chicago, 1957).
Ashton, T.S., *An Economic History of England: The Eighteenth Century*, (1955).
Black, Eugene C., *The Association* (Cambridge, Mass., 1963).
Boden, Ann, *William Hone's Political Journalism, 1815–1821* (University of Texas Ph.D. Thesis, 1975; University Microfilms, Ann Arbor, Michigan, 1979).
Brailsford, H.N., *Shelley, Godwin and their Circle* (Oxford, 1913).
Brown, P.A., *The French Revolution in English History* (1918).
Butler, Marilyn (ed.), *Burke, Paine, Godwin, and the French Revolution Controversy* (Cambridge English Prose Texts, 1984).
——, *Jane Austen and the War of Ideas* (Oxford, 1975).
——, *Peacock Displayed: A Satirist in his Context* (1979).
——, *Romantics, Rebels and Reactionaries: English Literature and its Background 1760–1830* (Oxford, 1981).
Carnall, Geoffrey, *Robert Southey and his Age* (1960).
Cobban, Alfred, *The Debate on the French Revolution, 1789–1800* (1950).
——, *Edmund Burke and the Revolt Against the Eighteenth Century* (1929).
Cohn, Albert M., *George Cruikshank: A Catalogue Raisonné of the work executed during the years 1806–1877* (1924).
Colmer, John, *Coleridge: Critic of Society* (Oxford, 1959).
Cone, C.B., *The English Jacobins* (New York, 1968).
Daiches, David, *Robert Burns and his World* (1971).
Emsley, C., *British Society and the French Wars, 1793–1815* (1979).
Erdman, David V., *Blake: Prophet Against Empire* (rev. 1969).
Godwin, A., *The Friends of Liberty* (1979).
Hone, J. Ann, *For the Cause of Truth: Radicalism in London, 1796–1821* (Oxford, 1982).
——, 'William Hone,' *Historical Studies* (October 1974).
Hackwood, Frederick William, *William Hone: His Life and Times* (London 1912, republished, New York, n.d.).

Jones, M.G., *Hannah More* (Cambridge, 1952).

Kelly, Gary, *The English Jacobin Novel, 1780–1805* (Oxford, 1976).

Lefebure, Molly, *The Bondage of Love: A life of Mrs Samuel Taylor Coleridge* (1986).

Legouis, Émile, *William Wordsworth and Annette Vallon* (1922).

Locke, Don, *A Fantasy of Reason* (1979).

McCalman, Iain, 'Unrespectable Radicalism: Infidels and Pornography in Early Nineteenth-Century London', *Past and Present*, No. 104, August 1984.

Macpherson, C.B., *Burke*, (1980).

Manuel, Frank E. and Fritzie P., *Utopian Thought in the Western World* (Oxford, 1979).

Mills, Howard, *Peacock: His Circle and his Age* (Cambridge, 1968).

Moorman, Mary, *William Wordsworth: A Biography*, 2 vols (Oxford, 1957).

O'Brien, Conor Cruise, 'Introduction' to Burke's *Reflections* (1968).

Paley, Morton D., *William Blake* (1978).

Palmer, R.R., *The Age of Democratic Revolution*, 2 vols (Princeton, 1959–64).

Paulson, Ronald, *Representations of Revolution (1789–1820)* (New Haven, 1983).

Prickett, Stephen (ed.), *The Romantics* (1981).

——, *Wordsworth and Coleridge: The Lyrical Ballads* (1975).

Reitzel, William (ed.), *The Autobiography of William Cobbett* (1967).

Smith, Olivia, *The Politics of Language, 1791–1819* (Oxford, 1984).

Spate, Virginia (ed.), *French Painting: The Revolutionary Decades 1760–1830* (Melbourne, 1980).

Spater, George, *William Cobbett: The Poor Man's Friend*, 2 vols (Cambridge, 1982).

Thomas, D.O., *The Honest Mind: The Thought and Work of Richard Price* (Oxford, 1977).

Thomis, M.I., and Holt, P., *Threats of Revolution in Britain, 1789–1848* (1977).

Thompson, E.P., *The Making of the English Working Class* (1965).

Todd, Janet (ed.), *A Dictionary of British and American Women Writers 1660–1800* (1984).

Tysdahl, B.J., *William Godwin as Novelist* (1981).

Willey, Basil, *The Eighteenth Century Background* (1940, repr. 1964).

Wynn-Jones, Michael, *George Cruikshank: His Life and London* (1978).

Index